DECISIONS IN THE DARK

DECISIONS IN THE DARK
A REFUGEE GIRL'S JOURNEY

EVA W. MAIDEN

Best wishes,
Eva W Maiden

BAY SOUND BOOKS
PALO ALTO, CALIFORNIA

Manufactured in the U.S.A.
BAY SOUND BOOKS
P.O. Box 60551
Palo Alto, CA 94306

Table of Contents

A Note to Readers

These stories come from vivid recollections of my early life that have stayed with me for many years.

Stories told to me by others appear in italics.

Introduction

I CAME TO THE United States as a refugee and tried to become an "American girl" in every way. When I was growing up, I didn't talk about the world I lived in before arriving here. By now, I am eager to share these stories. They come out of my precarious childhood and the difficult, contradictory situations of my youth. I wanted to write about each year as I saw it from the age I was at that time. As my writing continued, knots holding together family secrets became untied. It was a difficult process, but it had a freeing effect.

I was born in Vienna, Austria, the daughter of two busy Jewish physicians, with a brother five years older. Suddenly, as a preschooler I was the smallest of witnesses to the Nazi takeover of Austria. Hitler's goal was the annexation (*Anschluss*) of the nation of his birth, when he ordered the German troops to occupy Vienna in March, 1938. A hate campaign against the Jews was central to their military aim. As a little girl I felt the effects of the waves of terror that were swiftly imposed. We lived under threat at every moment. The Nazis stole everything from my family:

safety, possessions, work, school, a whole way of life.

Three quarters of a year later we escaped to Switzerland. Had we not fled, the four of us would have been targeted for death as part of the Nazi goal to eliminate all Jews from Europe. We were safe now, due to Swiss neutrality, but were separated as a family. Even when we reunited, my parents were not permitted to work or establish a home there. Shortly before the United States joined World War II, it became possible for us to immigrate to New York City.

It took my parents more than two years to learn English and study medicine in their new language. I'm proud that they became qualified to be healers again, to help others, and to improve our living conditions.

At the same time, the persecution and displacement that the family experienced left serious aftereffects. My brother and I had overwhelmed parents who coped poorly on the home front. They couldn't manage my brother, a difficult and traumatized child. And they were not prepared to give me the protection or direction that I needed. In time, my brother's deteriorating mental health created another kind of terror in my life. It seemed I was mostly going to have to raise myself.

As a ten-year-old child I began to set goals for myself. I began searching for new surroundings in which I could flourish. Somehow my strong inner resolve kept me on my path, in spite of many obstacles. Small kindnesses from others made a huge difference. The sources of support I was able to find in my teens shaped me as well.

By today, the members of my original family are no longer living. Along with facing their shortcomings I also hold their memory in affection and respect.

After college I was fortunate to have a long career in the field of mental health. As a school psychologist and psychotherapist, I often worked with children and families who had undergone trauma. When I saw people victimized by prejudice — or immigrants trying to make a new life — their struggles struck a familiar chord. In all of my work, I focused on helping people find their own strengths.

My Mother Dreams
of a Daughter

Vienna, Austria — 1934

MY MOTHER ANTONIA was a storyteller. It must have been deeply ingrained in her, coming from a rabbinical family where Chasidic stories were cherished. When I was a schoolchild and we were already in America, she enjoyed telling me the story of how my life began. Most often she was combing and braiding my hair in the morning as she spoke.

"When your brother Helmut turned four, your father and I felt it was time to have another child. You see, you were planned, and I especially wanted a daughter this time. I was almost forty, so now was the right time. We had money in the bank at last, even though it was still a hard time in Vienna. My pediatric practice was well established. Your father had a part-time job as a physician for the city of Vienna, and a part-time practice of his own. I figured my sister Valli and the nanny could deal with another baby. With the nursery and playroom right next to my office, I could supervise them closely."

Her face would be somber when she spoke of her mistakes. "I knew I had made mistakes with Helmut. Back in 1930, the medical books said a baby should be nursed every four hours on a schedule — when I think of all the crying he did in between, ach, that pains me. I was going to nurse the next baby whenever she was hungry, in between seeing patients. The other mistake was keeping my sister Otti, who was so severely retarded, in the apartment with us all these years. Poor Helmi had to compete with her for attention! This time I was going to place Otti in the Steinhof institution once and for all, no matter what my other three sisters would say!"

"Tell me more about Papi," I'd say.

"You know, I was disappointed in your father. He wasn't ambitious, like me. Can you imagine, he went to the Kaffeehaus almost every afternoon to shmooze and play chess with his buddy Dr. Lande? And when I was still weak from childbirth after your brother was born, he asked me to come in and assist him with a patient who had been in an accident! Oh, I have a long list of grudges, believe me. But, you know, I was a passionate woman, and I did love your father."

"Tell me again about when you met him!"

"Well, he was very shy when he was courting me. We met when we were classmates at University of Vienna. Anatomy class was very hard for me because we each had to cut up a cadaver. So Simon would come to the lab early and place a red rose on my cadaver! I'll never forget that.

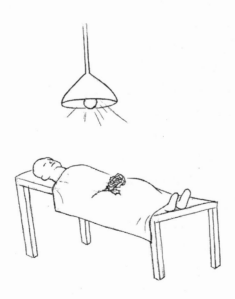

"While we were in medical school he got drafted as a medic in the First World War. He used to come over on the weekend to see me when he could. One time, to be with me, he even overstayed his leave and he got arrested!

"We finally got married when we completed our residencies a few years after World War I. My mother-in-law, your grandmother, didn't approve. She went around saying, 'Simondl is marrying five women!' just because I was so close to my sisters and they didn't have husbands. What did **she** know?"

"Tell me more about when I was born."

"Before you were born, I had a name picked out for you — Eva. That was the name of my favorite patient, Eva Landsman. Besides, Eva was the first woman, and I like to think that I was the first to do some things as a woman myself. For instance, that time I sued the University of Vienna! You see, my parents brought us five girls from Poland to Austria when I was 16. My father wanted to escape the pogroms, those terrible anti-Semitic riots in our town, and get a better education for me and Valli, his two youngest daughters. I entered *Gymnasium*, which is like high school in America, passed my *Matura* exam and applied at the university to go into medicine. It was a shock to me when I got a rejection letter. So I went to the Dean and said, 'I would like to know why my application was rejected when I had better grades than a number of my male classmates from the *Gymnasium* who were accepted.' He replied, 'It's simple. There are three reasons. You are a woman, you are a Jew, and you are stateless.' I told him, 'We'll see about that!' and left. Then I got a lawyer and sued for my admission, and the next year I got in. I'm never going to waste another year again!

"Well, you, my *Schatz*, came along in 1935, a daughter, as I hoped! Now we were well established and our family was complete. Ach, we couldn't have imagined what was coming!"

Observing My World

Age 2 ½

WHEN I WAS two and a half, my world was safe. I still remember the playroom I shared with my brother Helmut, five years older than me. He liked his tin soldiers best, and spinning a rubber toy on a string between two sticks, a game called Diabolo. My favorites were my doll Emily, and our shared teddy bear called *Pu der Bär* (Winnie the Pooh). In my bedroom was a crib, with a table for powder and cream after a bath. During the day my mother, Mutti, would pop in now and then to see me briefly. At night she bathed me and tucked me into bed with a lullaby: "*Schlaf, Kindlein, Schlaf.*" Mostly, we were tended by our nanny and Aunt Valli, my mother's sister who lived with us.

Tante Valli was so close to me that my earliest memory is of asking her: "Are you a parent?" I was trying to figure out if I had three parents, while in the stories that I listened to there were only two. Valli was always available while my mother and father were busy in their medical offices. She was nervously cheerful as she bustled between supervising the household help and admitting patients at the door: child patients coming to see my mother, adults to see my father.

My father, Papi, usually smiled whenever he saw me. He liked to tell me interesting things about the world, speaking in a soft tone of voice. He was different from some other fathers I knew who only seemed to talk to their children about how to behave right.

On weekdays I went to Tante Pia's nursery school, a very happy place for me. My coat had a little snail embroidered inside, and my locker had a painting of that snail, so I always knew where to hang my coat after my nanny dropped me off. Tante Pia, a tiny woman with a deformed back, showed a warm and sensible authority. I loved her. I remember standing in line with the other bundled-up children on our rooftop playground, getting ready to sing in a circle and play games.

On the weekend my family and my father's relatives sometimes went to visit Omama, my one grandparent. She was a bit stricter and more serious than my parents, but I liked seeing her and played happily there, sometimes with my two older girl cousins. My father was always so pleased to see his brothers at Omama's house.

Mutti was affectionate only with her own sisters. After Tante Valli, my second favorite was Tante Ida, whom we called Edie. She was a seamstress, and used to make cute dresses for me and nice

17

linen things for my mother. Her visits to our apartment were a treat.

Helmut sometimes liked to play with me, but at other times he called me a pest. His special name for me was Nuni, never Eva. When I asked why, he said, "When you were born, I was having a book read to me called 'Nuni Among the Giants.' With all the grown-ups fussing over you, I thought of you as the little Nuni." The name stuck forever.

The Anschluss

March, 1938

*I*N MARCH, 1938, a significant number of Austrian Nazi party members were already prepared
for the takeover by Germany. The entering German
troops were welcomed as if it was a great holiday
parade, with bystanders waving swastika flags and
giving the Nazi salute. As young as I was, that day
has stayed in my memory. Immediately afterwards
a coercive election was held and Austria was merged
into Germany.

My nanny told me that today was a grand occasion, her plump cheeks flushed with excitement. She dressed me up in my best clothes and said we would be going out. Somebody important had arrived, and everyone was supposed to watch the parade and greet him. When I was dressed she brought me to the living room to say goodbye to my parents. But when we entered the room, my mother was very cross, her face pale and angry. She scolded the nanny in a loud voice, saying that the children would NOT be going out today. Then she ordered her to change me to my play clothes. She warned my brother and me that we were not to go out on the balcony of our second story apartment UNDER ANY CIRCUMSTANCES. Then she pulled the red velvet drapes shut, something she usually did only at night. My stomach felt as if it was falling. Mutti's words, the fear in her voice — Papi so quiet and sad, looking into the distance — what was going on?

My brother Helmut, a highly active and mischievous boy, seemed unusually quiet that day. I figured that with his being five years older, as he often reminded me, he knew the reasons for things that I didn't understand. His best friend Lito, a classmate and neighbor in the building, had fashioned a wooden freight train of flat cars for me. He had painted each one in a different color, with my nickname on it: **Nuni.** Helmut and I ran the train listlessly over the Persian carpets for hours that day.

Shortly afterwards my father reported to his part-time job as usual. He had been a medical examiner and public health physician for the City of Vienna for many years. As he walked into the office, he was shocked to find his boss in full Nazi uniform. This physician was the same man who had been a guest at my brother's bris (circumcision ceremony for a boy baby). At that time he presented a gift of his own father's pocket watch, saying, "Since my wife and I can't have children, we would like your son to have this." But now, as soon as he saw my father arriving at work, he said to the secretary, "Did that Jew still come to work here? No Jews are to return to government jobs under the Third Reich!" My father was 43 years old at the time. It is said that his hair turned white overnight after this betrayal.

Only a little later my father received a call from a patient of his, a secretary at the city police headquarters. "Herr Doktor, I just typed a list of men to be arrested tomorrow, and your name was on the list! They are arresting Social Democrats and Jews. You have got to disappear!" Immediately my father thought of his medical school colleague, Dr. Lande. Until recently, they often met in the afternoon at a local Kaffeehaus. The two men talked the situation over covertly and it was agreed that my father could hide in a pantry cabinet at the Landes' kitchen while the situation was "hot." Dr. Lande was Catholic and his wife was very pious. When the Nazis or the Austrian

police went on door-to-door searches, she would an-
swer their knock holding her rosary beads and scold
them for disturbing her at prayer. They would move
on quickly. Later my father would come home again
until the next warning.

Soon after the Anschluss, Nazi teachers had
taken over every classroom in Helmut's elementary
school. When I was old enough to understand, my
parents told me why my brother came home from
school sobbing on the first day and cried all after-
noon. The new Nazi teacher had singled out his pal
Lito, who was also Jewish, for punishment. He was
locked in the coat closet for the entire day. My brother
said that when he tried to approach the closet, he
was told he would be given the same treatment and
had to back away.

Life Under Nazi Occupation

THE GROWN-UPS in the house changed a lot, looking very worried and telling secrets I wasn't supposed to hear. Even when I was in the same room with Mutti and Papi they acted almost as if I wasn't there. Only my Aunt Valli was still her cheerful and affectionate self. Fewer patients were coming to the door to see my parents, and after a while, almost none. I wondered why my father disappeared from time to time, or where he went, but I clearly wasn't supposed to ask.

After a while I wasn't in nursery school any more. My mother told me it was closed now. She took me with her each day to stand in a different line, usually a couple of blocks long, while she waited to see a consul. The words "affidavit" and "visa" were used a lot but I didn't know what they meant. I felt very tired on those long days, and complained my feet were hurting. Mutti told me that we had to keep waiting. I figured a consul was sort of like the king of a country, as in fairy tales. I understood that my mother was asking permission to go to his country, that is, if we reached the front of the line before the office closed. She always ended up looking sad, so it seemed that they were saying "no" each time.

I knew the other people in the line were Jews like us who were trying to get out and go somewhere else. Why did people hate us now? Had we done something wrong? I often thought about the terrifying German children's book *Struwwelpeter* that showed bad things happening to people because they had bad habits or had misbehaved. But what had we done that was bad? There was no way to ask adults such a question. It was pretty hard to get them to answer any questions at all.

Jewish children were now barred from public schools. Their parents had a choice of keeping them at home or sending them to a Jewish school, facing the danger of their being harassed or beaten on the way, often with no one to come to their rescue. My brother began to attend a Jewish school. I never heard any details about his walking to school and back, but I believe that he was tormented along the way.

One day, the Jewish women in our building were dragged out of their apartment homes by Nazi officers and were ordered to scrub the cobblestones in front of the house with toothbrushes. My mother and Aunt Valli were on their hands and knees scrubbing under armed guard when a Catholic woman from the building next door spoke out in anger: "What is this!

Don't you realize this woman is our Frau Doktor?" She quickly walked over to my mother and picked her up, pulling her into the safety of her own apartment. They waited together until that day of slave labor and humiliation was over, and my mother returned home to her exhausted sister. My mother often repeated this story of the neighbor who risked her life, taking a stand against hatred.

That summer, a serious epidemic of scarlet fever was spreading among the children of Vienna. By this time, no Jewish doctor was allowed to practice or have hospital privileges, nor did Gentile doctors attend Jewish children. My mother decided to take an action that would have been too dangerous for her male colleagues. Each evening, she would take a stroll after dinner carrying her large black "purse," actually a medical bag. Her "visits" were house calls, not only to her own patients, but to those of other Jewish pediatricians. Years later I met several Austrian refugee children who recognized our name and told me that my mother was the pediatrician who saved their lives that summer.

Two Arrests I
Learned of Later

*O*NE DAY EARLY *in the fall of 1938, two German soldiers came to arrest my mother. I came to the door and they say I greeted them cheerfully. I'm told that I even called out "Soldiers, soldiers!" as if I was pleased to see them. When I was older I learned that they took my mother downstairs and put her in a truck with a group of women, headed in the direction of the outskirts of the city – the Vienna Woods. At a rest stop for the soldiers, one of them said of my mother: "This one's pretty, let her go." She was pushed off the truck and left behind as it drove to an unknown destination. By the time she had hiked home it was almost morning.*

In November 1938, during the week of the Kristallnacht *pogrom, a huge anti-Semitic riot was about to begin. On the "night of shattered glass" the Nazis in Vienna smashed Jewish shops, burned synagogues, and arrested Jewish men on the streets. Just before that night our nanny, seemingly ignorant of dangers, took my brother Helmut to the Prater. This was the park that Viennese children loved for* its giant Ferris wheel. How could she have missed the signs on the park benches that said "Jews Unwelcome" or "No Dogs or Jews Allowed?" She sat on a bench while Helmut played nearby. Suddenly a Nazi officer appeared and said to my eight-year-old brother, "You're under arrest for being on the grass!"

Helmut was taken to jail. Somehow the officer knew he was Jewish, though he looked like any other Austrian schoolboy with his blonde hair and green eyes, wearing the typical lederhosen (leather pants). Our family learned later that he was taken to a cell and tortured. We know only that the officers beat him, and repeated over and over, "Tell us where your parents keep their gold!" My mother waited in desperation in the lobby of the police station until he was released that night. All he said to her then was, "I thought I would never see you again."

My brother never recovered from the agony of that day. He was changed forever. I didn't hear the story of his arrest until I was six. I think I had already noticed that his moods were different – often he was very subdued, and at other times, easily enraged.

The Escape

IT WAS DECEMBER and we were going to leave Vienna after all! I was told that we were going to Switzerland, a country that had many large mountains and NO NAZIS. My father even smiled sometimes these days, telling us he would study English and teach it to us while we waited in Zürich for a visa to America. According to the German rules, we were each allowed to pack a box of a very specific size. My mother humorously called these the matzoh boxes — the size was about the same as the kind that held enough matzohs for all of Passover. I could already see that there might not be enough room for *Pu der Bär* (Winnie the Pooh), but I was determined that my doll Emily would escape with us.

My parents' bank accounts had been declared the property of the German Reich. Jews were also forbidden to take jewelry or more than just a few schillings out of the country. Yet the official Nazi policy at that time was to pressure Jews to emigrate.

Mutti cried a lot on the day we were to leave while talking about her three sisters still being in danger in Vienna. I was sobbing too, because we were leaving Tante Valli behind. In the hour before we left, my mother dressed me in a summer dress and put some of her necklaces on me. Then she put my fall dress over that, with several shiny pins; and over that, my winter dress and coat. She told me in a very serious voice that I was to stay close to her and above all, avoid being patted by anyone.

At the airport, I could hear my mother asking my father over and over, "Do you have all the documents?" But my own thoughts were about how to stay beyond arm's reach of the men in Nazi uniforms. At the door of the plane, I started to panic when the soldier standing near us re-checked our papers and said I was very cute. Luckily he didn't touch me, and the four of us were seated. When the plane left the ground, my father's face was as white as his hair. My brother vomited on and off throughout the trip, while a kindly stewardess attended to him. I began to think of Aunt Valli and *Pu der Bär* and started wailing, "Where's the door? I want to go home!" Mutti hushed me, but I kept repeating and repeating the same words.

Finally the plane landed in Switzerland, and my mother said, "*Gott sei dank* (Thank you God)." Suddenly, there was a new shock. Two men in white uniforms came with a stretcher to take my father off the plane and put him in an ambulance! I didn't even know he was sick! Mutti finally explained: "Papi needs an operation. They're taking him to the hospital right away. We arranged this in advance." *(For fear of being arrested my father had delayed an appendectomy. It would have been dangerous for him to be admitted to a hospital in Vienna, even one where he had recently been on the staff.)*

After my mother, brother and I stepped out of the plane, I explained to my doll that no one was trying to kill us, here in Switzerland.

Our Arrival in Switzerland

December, 1938

OUR RABBI COUSIN greeted us at the Zürich airport in an awkward manner. His wild eyes and long beard discomforted me. He got a taxi to take my mother, brother and me home with him for a night. I felt a little better after his wife served us dinner.

My cousin's bed and his wife's bed had been pushed together, and I was put to sleep on the crack between the two. I wasn't used to sleeping with grown-ups and these people didn't seem at all cuddly. I lay awake for a long time in discomfort and fear. The next morning after breakfast, the rabbi's wife sent the three of us to a *pension*, a kind of boardinghouse. The lady in charge there had an annoying habit of saying, "*Ja, so...*" very often yet never chatting. She told my mother in a rude way that we could only stay two weeks.

I noticed a beautifully decorated Christmas tree standing in the living room of the pension and wished I could sneak in to see the little hanging toys up close, but she repeated over and over that we children were not to enter the room. I could see that this lady didn't like any of us, and I wondered if she thought I was still a baby who broke things. Or did she think my mother's troubles might be catching, like a disease?

Our two weeks there were almost up when my mother told me that a Swiss Jewish agency that helped refugees had found a place for us to live. There would be just enough room for two people. My father was staying at the convalescent home so we were three — how could this work? Mutti said there wasn't enough space or food for Helmut, so he was to go to a *Kinderheim* (orphanage). I tried to argue with her, but it didn't do any good. I had never imagined that she could bear to send one of us away. I wondered to myself if she would send me away too, some day.

My mother and I moved into a small room in the apartment of the Horn family on Stockerstrasse. They were an older couple with two grown-up sons and a daughter, Thelma. They had to crowd up together to make enough space for Mutti and me. They were Jewish in rather a stricter way than we were, even about what to wear. Once, the old man punished me for wearing a short-sleeved dress instead of a long-sleeved one. Nobody told me about that rule before, and besides, I was pretty sure God didn't mind short sleeves.

Many weeks after we arrived here I still kept asking Mutti when my brother and my father would be with us again. She answered that it might be a long time till my brother Helmut got out of the orphanage and Papi came back from the place for people whose operations didn't go right. Mutti said I shouldn't worry—they were safe now, and would join us someday when we got a bigger place to stay, or when we got visas to go to America.

A Birthday Celebration

April, 1939

It seemed to me there were two kinds of kids here — "regular" kids, and *"Emigranteli,"* as the Swiss called us. So I was surprised when Thelma Horn told me she was planning to take me somewhere special for my fourth birthday. We were going to see a play! Wasn't that something only "regular" kids did? I watched her face closely, and it did look as if she really meant it. Maybe on the way we would stop to buy marzipan candies shaped like colorful fruits, the kind I stared at in the shop windows every day, almost tasting their delicious sweetness.

When the day came, Mutti dressed me in my Austrian *dirndl* (folk dress) and took a long time brushing my hair. She gave me instructions about being polite at the theater and making sure to thank Thelma. I heard Thelma calling me to help her tighten her corset as she was dressing in the next room. It wasn't an easy job, as she had a super large body, but at least she smelled good.

At last we arrived at the theater and sat down in the middle of a very excited crowd. When the curtain went up, a mean sort of mother was onstage making her daughter work very hard. The girl was tired and fell into a well. At the bottom, she landed in a different world. A very kind woman named Mother Holle lived there. She showed the little girl how to clean the house, but never made her hurry or punished her for mistakes.

One day Mother Holle showed the girl her special magic trick. When it was time to air the feather beds by hanging them over the balcony, the way Swiss women did, she gave them an extra shake. Out came a very large bunch of feathers, and right away, they turned into snow!

I screamed with delight along with the other children when the feathers turned into snowflakes. Mother Holle was explaining how she created the seasons. She let the little girl try the trick, and it worked for her, too.

Was it really possible to jump into a different world, where people were not mean? I was four now, and I wanted to understand things. Many people were nice to me in Switzerland, but my mother was mostly sad and complained a lot that nobody cared about us.

One Sunday a month my mother and I took a long train ride to visit my brother Helmut. He seemed so scared! He told us the people at the orphanage were mean to him. He hated being away from us, and it broke my heart when he cried and asked to be taken "home." It was confusing, too, because we didn't exactly *have* a home. On a different Sunday we would take the train in the opposite direction and visit my father at his bedside. Papi said the nurses who took care of him were good to him, and he was better. He didn't really look better, though, from one visit to the next.

It was hard for me to fall asleep at night in the little room with my mother. I wondered and worried about many things with my eyes wide open. It even occurred to me that maybe it would have been better if I had been the one to be sent away — I could get used to things more easily than Helmut could. Before finally falling asleep, I would give my feather comforter a special shake for good luck — just in case.

Chestnuts

I can still smell the chestnut trees as they were when their leaves had fallen and chestnuts began to drop. I would take a long walk with my parents, holding one of each of their hands. Then I would run ahead. They would act surprised — "What a fast one!" they would say as my four-year-old legs dashed forward, leaves crunching under my feet. If I stopped to pick up chestnuts on the street and lagged behind they would call out, "Come on, little snail!"

What joy to have my father back! I had missed him so much. It was good to have my brother back, too. The constant stomachache I used to have was gone now that they were with us again. Only one thing could spoil a lovely walk with my parents. The sight of a policeman in uniform would make me tremble all over. It didn't matter how often Mutti and Papi would tell me policemen were safe here in Zürich. I really couldn't be sure. Large dogs terrified me as well, especially German shepherds, the kind I had seen on the streets in Vienna.

The chestnuts felt smooth and cool in my hand and fit into the apron pockets of my *dirndl*. I gave them to my parents pretending we could eat them. Actually, my mother often didn't have money for the food she wanted to buy for us. It was upsetting for me to listen to her when she had to go to see a social worker and beg for more food or money. The family we lived with was not responsible for our meals. Sometimes I played on the kitchen floor close to their dinnertime so that Frau Horn just couldn't help inviting me to dinner.

When the Horn family finally decided to let Papi and Helmut join us after all, I believed that it was because of me. I had overheard my mother asking a social worker for a larger place to live. When Mutti mentioned this to Frau Horn, she replied that they could not bear to have **me** leave — why not just bring over the rest of the family, they'd manage it somehow.

After a while my mother got a job in a chocolate factory. I wasn't allowed to talk about it. I guess it was a secret because refugees weren't supposed to work. I sort of liked the days when we had just candy for dinner, though our cook in Vienna would have disapproved, and so would my nanny. It was brave of Mutti to steal candy from the factory where she worked. If I had two hungry children, I would have done it too, in spite of what Tante Leni told us at nursery school about not stealing. My mother would take the chocolates out of her apron pockets and give them to me and my brother. The chocolates were called "bed-hoppers" because we had to jump into bed before we could have them. After that Mutti would tuck us in.

On our walks, my mother would point out red flowers hanging from a window or balcony as if she was under a spell from the beauty of Zürich. I felt mixed up when she did that. How could she love this place, when very often she had to visit the *Fremdenpolizei* (alien police office), with me tagging along? There, a very nasty man asked her questions. "Why are you still here, Doctor? Isn't it about time you had a visa for America and took off?" She would always have an answer — she was good at these things — but I could feel her shaking. The man stamped some sort of paper, and then we would leave till next time.

Often my family's destination on walks was Zürich See, the wonderful lake in the park. I loved watching the swans gliding across the water. My nursery school went there during the week, too. My friend Georgie and I would tease the swans as they walked on the grass. It was very hard to decide whether to feed the swans a piece of bread the way other children did. Giving up that slice from the school lunch bag might mean being hungrier in the evening. But sometimes it was worth it!

Nowadays we only saw our rabbi cousin at his synagogue, from the distance of the balcony where the women and girls sat on Saturday mornings. I wished I could like him, because I now understood that he was the one who had sent for us and got us out of Vienna. But my mother was angry with him because he never invited us to his home, and I continued to feel scared around him.

My safest place was among my friends in Tante Leni's nursery school class. Pierre was the smallest boy. He always wore a beret and did not smile. Tante Leni specially asked me to be nice to him because "his parents didn't get out with him." When we stood in line to go indoors I made sure to stand next to him. Once, Georgie and I got into mischief together when our class went on a trip to the museum. It was hot as the group stood around waiting for the streetcar to bring us back. There was a beautiful fountain in front of the museum, and I talked Georgie into jumping into the shallow water with me. We splashed around and cooled off. We were very happy, despite the scolding we got and our dripping all over the streetcar on the way back.

Of course Zürich was beautiful. But we didn't have a home anymore. I felt uncomfortable with all four of us living in a small room in the Stocker-strasse apartment. We didn't get along well enough with each other to live so close together. My father kept saying, some day soon we would go to America, he could be a doctor again, and we would have an apartment of our own.

An Arrest After
We Left Vienna

*M*Y AUNT VALLI *stayed behind in our apartment in Vienna after we left. A natural optimist, she believed that the Nazis would be gone in due time. Meanwhile she could maintain the apartment on Taborstrasse with its offices and our family quarters. A Nazi woman doctor showed up from Germany one day, and announced that she was moving in and taking over my parents' medical practices. Valli could stay as her unpaid maid and receptionist for the time being — in other words, her slave. Although Valli hated her, the situation fit in with her plan.*

Some months later, as part of the Nazis' relentless actions against "inferior races," there was a roundup of the gypsies of Vienna and Aunt Valli was arrested along with them. While in jail, she made a defiant remark to a guard. He immediately yelled at her: "Shut your animal jowl, or we'll send you right to the camps." As Valli described it, this was the first time she really felt the danger of her situation, having believed that only men went to concentration camps. The next day men and women alike were taken from their cells and loaded onto trucks to be moved somewhere — no one knew the destination. A Nazi officer methodically checked off their names. When he came to the name "Valerie Marie Taubes" he roared, "That woman's no gypsy! Get her out of here!"

Once on the street, Aunt Valli immediately made plans to leave Austria. She went to ask for help at the Viennese communal Jewish agency, the Kultusgemeinde, *where her father (my grandfather) had worked years ago. Through them, she obtained a job as a nanny in New York — and with the job, a letter stating that her employer would be her financial sponsor. Now she was ready to visit the American consulate, where she had received a low number in the lottery for the scarce visas some months ago. Her visa came through for December, 1939. Before leaving, she had flowers delivered to us in Zürich with a note that only my mother could decipher according to a code they had agreed upon. She indicated that she was on the move and that their two sisters in Vienna were all right so far. A letter was to follow.*

When my aunt arrived in New York in 1939, she went straight to her live-in job. She got on well with her employer. The whole household used to giggle when Aunt Valli reported that she had heard from us, saying, "I became a letter." Aunt Valli was fortunate that the pediatrician of her young charges was Dr. Benjamin Spock. He liked her way with children, and soon told her he would see to it that she was never without a job.

My aunt, who was not a gypsy, nonetheless had wandered far and now was ready to gather her clan. She devoted her weekly day off to finding ways for my parents, my brother and I to get to America. She must have told our story in her meager English to many social agencies and charitable American Jews: her sister and brother-in-law, both physicians, were stuck in Switzerland but would never be permitted to work there; sometimes they couldn't even feed their two children. The Hebrew Immigrant Aid Society in New York, known as HIAS, added us to their list. Valli stayed in touch with my father's two brothers, recent refugees themselves who were now living in Providence, Rhode Island with their families. Through their local rabbi, my uncles eventually were able to arrange for most of the documents we needed. In the spring of 1940 Valli secured the help of Walter Haas, Sr. in New York to pay for our ship's passage. Ours was to be the last passenger ship to leave Italy before America joined the war.

Voyage to America on the S.S. Rex

Genoa, Italy — May, 1940

WE ALL STOOD in the harbor in Genoa, gazing at the enormous ship in wonder: Mutti, Papi, Helmut, and Omama (my grandmother). Last week we had stayed for a week or so in Omama's small apartment in Milan, where she was staying with two other Austrian widows. I didn't understand how Omama got to Italy from Vienna, but I was getting used to the idea that everyone important to me went someplace else.

Omama liked Italy, and was charming when she spoke Italian, as if it softened her somehow. She had taken us on some fine walks through Milan, showing us beautiful buildings and sculptures. In between lively talks, she sometimes had fear on her face — as if a shadow was passing over it.

Today she had joined us all on the train to Genoa to meet the S.S. Rex. I was thrilled that we actually had tickets for America! As we stood on the dock I looked at my father and saw that the rosy color had faded from his face. He put his arm around Omama and said, "I'm so sorry, Mother, so very sorry that we have no visa for you! We tried what we could, but you know how hard it has been for just the four of us to get visas and affidavits for America. I'm afraid for you, in Italy."

Omama stayed calm. She replied, "Don't worry, Simondl, God will take care of me." At that moment I realized that she had her own personal connection to God, which my parents did not seem to have. I wished I could just take her hand and pull her along with us.

Looking around the Genoa harbor, I saw many men in black shirts, just as I had noticed in Milan. It puzzled me: a black shirt wasn't exactly a uniform, yet it seemed like one, all the same. I knew, though I wasn't supposed to know, that the men in black shirts could someday kill Omama. I recognized a certain look on their faces, as I had seen it on men wearing uniforms in Vienna.

By now we had reached the front of the line and it was time to get onboard the ship. The ship's horn blew on a sad yet exciting note. We each gave a final hug to Omama and climbed the staircase to the lowest deck. My mother went off to the cabin while we children stood with our father on the deck along with hundreds of other people, many of them shabby and forlorn. At last we caught sight of Omama and waved our handkerchiefs, and she returned the wave with hers. I set my mind to remember her face forever, the way she smelled of lemons, and her pet name for me, *Mein Goldenes Kind* (my golden child). My father was weeping. I had never seen him cry before.

After we explored our very small cabin, Helmut and I began to wander around the ship. He explained to me that there were rich people on the upper deck, and after a day at sea we sneaked up at mealtime to see what they were having to eat. We also checked out the ship's store, where I fell in love with a fuzzy teddy bear the size of my middle finger. His arms and legs moved despite his tiny size, and he seemed perfect for living in my pocket. Later, while I was asking my mother if she would buy him, I felt guilty. The answer was as I expected: "We have no money, what are you thinking!"

After a few days the adventure began to feel like a long confinement. My brother was frequently seasick, and became more and more irritable. Any of the few toys we had with us were claimed by him, and he ordered me not to play with them.

Once, when he was away from the cabin, I began to play with a toy that we'd had in our playroom in Vienna a long time ago. Helmut came back into the cabin and was immediately filled with rage. "I told you not to play with anything, you old *kaput*-maker," he screamed. "You spoil everything!" Then he picked up a shoe from the floor and threw it at my head with such force that I felt sure some part of my face was broken. I was in shock, perhaps less from being hurt than from amazement that my own brother would harm me this way.

After that, it was never the same between us. My parents tended to me and scolded him mildly that day, but I knew this was very different from the way other brothers and sisters quarrel. I was not going to be safe, not even in America!

A few days later, we neared the harbor at last. My father awakened me to step out and see the Statue of Liberty from the deck, a thrilling sight. Soon we were part of a pushing throng of people who looked a lot happier than when they had boarded. And it seemed in New York you didn't have to queue up in such an orderly way.

Every moment of not seeing Aunt Valli on the dock was an anxious one — but suddenly she appeared, bursting with smiles and laden with packages. First she gave us each as big a hug as possible, and then she gushed to us children: "You're gonna love America! I brought you stuff you've never tasted — white bread and Pepsi-Cola! You wouldn't believe the things they eat here!" To our parents, she explained that she had rented one room in Washington Heights for us, but there would be an apartment available soon. After we somehow got connected with our luggage, our new life began with a taxi ride. I liked America already.

How Do You Like America?

New York, NY

IWAS IN FIRST GRADE, and very glad that I could speak English. When I started school, I didn't even know how to ask to go to the bathroom! Now I could sing American songs and was starting to read books. After school, I walked about a mile to our apartment, usually with a friend or two. It felt good to walk in and get a hug from each of my parents right away. They were studying English, each teaching the other how to say English words — with a German accent. We all had fits of laughter about things they had to memorize from their lesson book, like "If mouses are mice, why aren't houses hice?" At dinner, they spoke German, but now I answered in English.

We had enough food these days. Now and then my mother would leave our neighborhood, Washington Heights, and take the subway to the Jewish Board of Guardians to ask for more money for our family. I would come along, and was instructed to tell the social worker that everything was fine. The particular things I was not to mention were that my brother hit me very hard sometimes, or that my father worked in a sports club at night, giving massages.

My mother took me to other places, too, when she had business to take care of. Sometimes I helped her say things in English. Often the grownups we met asked me, "How do you like America?" To be polite, I answered "I like it very much," which was true. Of course it was wonderful to be here, in a city where all kinds of people seemed to be welcome. But I was surprised Americans could ask such a silly question, as if we picked a nice spot out of a magazine. Didn't they understand that we came here to escape great danger in Austria, and to live in a place where my parents could work, not like Switzerland?

It was always a good day when Aunt Valli came home on her day off from her job as a nanny. Sometimes when she and I went to Woolworth's she gave me a nickel or dime to buy something I wanted. She always cooked a good dinner and told us stories about her latest *panya* (Polish for employer) and the baby she was caring for.

At night when my brother and I played, each of us used a comforter to make a fort. He played war a lot of the time, but I didn't think about it much until the day of the big newspaper headlines and excitement. "America is going to join the war," my father said. "Now more Jews can be saved, and we can get rid of Hitler!" My parents seemed happy and yet sad at the same time. My father still had cousins in Austria, and my mother, in Poland. What would the declaration of war mean for them?

One day, a package came from Vienna. How was that possible? Who had sent it? We hadn't gotten letters from relatives there since we came to New York. As I was about to ask, my brother had already opened the package and announced, "My toys are here!" I saw a couple of toys and books that had belonged to me in our playroom and said, "Some of them are mine" while reaching for them. This led to a really big beating, so hard my body will never forget it. My parents tried to get him off me, but I guess they weren't strong enough.

I started to stay out on the street longer after school, when the weather was good enough. The girls' games were fun — hopscotch and jump rope were my favorites. Somehow, games where a ball was coming in my direction scared me and I couldn't play them right. The ball reminded me of a fist coming at me and I often just scrunched my eyes instead of hitting it.

Yes, of course I liked America. I wanted to be just like American girls in every way I could, though it wasn't always possible — for one thing, my clothes didn't look quite like those of the other girls. And I couldn't go "over the hill and around the bend to grandmother's house" as in the story my teacher was reading to the class. All the same, I was determined to "fit in."

Morning in
Washington Heights

IT'S ALWAYS THE SAME song on the radio that wakes me up: "Pack up your troubles in your old kit bag and smile, smile, smile…" I hope today will be a smiling day! I wiggle out of my pajamas and put on my undershirt, panties, and the dress that came out of the CARE package a while back. It's getting a little tight on me. Now I have to do my job: turning the bed back into the green couch. I strip off the sheets and sort of fold them with my comforter. They go into the closet, and then the heavy bolsters go from the floor to the couch. Now the apartment has a living room again.

Papi is still sleeping and Helmut is hogging the bathroom. Aunt Valli has left to go to her nanny job. I like being alone in the kitchen with Mutti. Her face has a special glow reflecting the orange light of the electric burner beneath the glass coffeemaker. I think she loves having her own kitchen after the years when we didn't have our own home. She fixes hot cereal and then makes my sandwich for lunch and stuffs it into a brown bag.

The best part of the morning is when my mother

brushes my long hair and slowly makes two braids. It's a good time for talking. Her hair is straight and black, pulled back into a bun. She says she likes it that mine is brown and wavy. She tells me that she is learning American English from talking with me! Her book for English class is from England, and it's different from how they talk here.

I've been saving up a question. "Could you sign a paper for me to have a free lunch at school? I see the kids eating hot lunches, and they look very good." "Oh no, *Schatzi*, that's for poor people and we aren't poor!" Then she slips rubber bands over the ends of my braids.

I roll her words around in my mind. Just in the last week I heard Mutti and Papi talking about how to budget the money that came from the refugee groups like the Jewish Board of Guardians. They decided to divide the money three ways: one part for our family, one part to try to rescue relatives who were still in Vienna, and one part to buy medical books for my parents to study — as soon as their English is good enough. Since I heard that, I've been worrying about whether we will have enough money to buy things. I hope it's true that we're not really poor.

It's time to dash down the four flights of steps to go outside and head over to school. I pass the Shapiros' apartment on the second floor where I sometimes ring the bell. Like me, they speak both

German and English. They have so many children that usually one of them can play with me.

Once, when I was by myself on the way to school, I got lost — I was so mixed up that I forgot how to ask directions in English! Finally I went into a store to warm up, and the nice storekeeper helped me. Today I see another girl from my school, P.S.169, and catch up with her. We walk the ten city blocks together.

Warmth in Winter

I WAS EXCITED to start second grade at P.S. 169, but my feelings changed very soon. My teacher insisted that the whole class needed to be working on the same page at all times, or at least sit still with hands folded. I had finished the year's work in my textbooks at home during the first month of school. Now I wanted to figure out solutions to many mysterious problems. I wanted to read books with chapters that told about faraway places. After all, I spoke English well, after two years in the United States. But even if I was still in Austria, I was sure I'd be reading fairy tales, which I loved, even the scary ones, and not baby stuff like what my teacher gave us.

My parents were very busy at home studying medical books in English, often with a colleague or two from Vienna, in which case I had to be extra quiet. It was important not to disturb them, because the sooner they finished their examinations, the sooner they could work again.

Helmut now attended Edward W. Stitt Junior High School in a very rough neighborhood, and seemed sad or angry all the time. I often felt a sense of terror when I was near him, as he might go on a hitting rampage at any time. When he pummeled me, I would be sore for days.

One day as the weather was getting colder, I ducked into the public library on St. Nicholas Avenue to warm up on my way home from school. There was a large, pleasant space for children, and the colors and smells of books felt inviting. I watched other children asking the librarian questions, and decided to ask her mine: did they have any books about girls who lived in other countries? "Oh, yes, many," she said smiling. After getting my own library card, I brought home an armful of books, and was back the next week. "Do you mind if I read fairy tales?" I asked this time. I confided that my teacher had told me I must read "second grade books" only. "Your teacher is wrong," she said, and we began an exploration that took up many full afternoons after school.

An embarrassing thing happened to me at school with winter approaching. I was sent to the principal for shivering! It seemed shameful and funny at the same time. The school principal hoisted up her skirt and showed me her long underpants. She explained, "This is what we wear in America to keep warm." What made me laugh inside was that my mother had told me Swiss winter underwear was the best in the world. I wasn't about to tell the principal that I had outgrown my Swiss winter clothes and there wasn't money for new ones.

Around the same time, the librarian asked me
if I would call her "Aunt Belle." Yes, of course she
could be a sort of aunt! It was so nice that she wanted this, even if it was a little awkward. My eyes got
teary, as I remembered overhearing my mother say
that maybe the Nazis had killed my aunts in Austria
by now. America is a place, it seemed, that gives
you aunts instead of taking them away.

By December, I started staying past the time I
was supposed to come home from the library. My
father or mother would walk a few blocks to the library to remind me that it was time for dinner. Even
my brother came a few times. He could be quite responsible on the rare occasions when he was supposed to be in charge of me. Aunt Belle took time

to get to know each family member a little bit when they stopped in, always telling them something good about me.

Close to the end of the year, Aunt Belle told me in an excited voice that she had a big Christmas package for my whole family. One of my parents would need to stop by and pick it up. She told me that she had met a family where the father was the same size as my father, the daughter the same size as me, and so on — and they had given her clothes that they were tired of! I marveled at this amazing good luck. For once, I couldn't wait to go home, as I was eager to tell my family about the surprise.

My father came with me the next day and carried off the huge bundle, with many gracious thank-you's. When we opened it at home and each of us tried on the warm winter clothes, everything was a perfect fit. My mother asked me to repeat Aunt Belle's explanation about the package and then said in German something like "that's some story." I ignored her, but thinking about it a few weeks later, I could imagine that the librarian might have searched hard to find these clothes, and maybe there wasn't really any family with just our sizes.

Aunt Belle's kindness made me comfortable all through that winter, and so did the safety and warmth of the library.

News of Omama
1943

SOMETIMES I PICTURED my grandmother waving goodbye to us in my mind, even in my dreams. My father had begun to worry about her much more. Finally the Red Cross sent him news: she had escaped from Italy to Switzerland!

When she was able to write to my father she told about hiding in a church in Milan when the German troops first came to Italy. The priest was known to be friendly toward Italian and foreign Jews. At first, she and others who had taken refuge there thought the church would be a safe hiding place. Then reports came that the Nazis were beginning to raid churches in search of Jews, with a plan to deport them to concentration camps. The priest told Omama to pack her belongings in a knapsack quickly. Omama wrote with pride that she had managed to stuff the silver candlesticks, the ones she used every Friday night with Sabbath prayers, into her knapsack. The priest arranged for a guide to drive her close to the Swiss border to a place where she could secretly enter on foot — with no documents.

She was able to hike into Switzerland unseen,

evading border guards and clambering around the unfamiliar terrain. After some days she was arrested and brought to a detention center. There the Red Cross was assisting undocumented immigrants.

I remember how her letters were punctuated with two favorite abbreviations: G.S.D. stood for "*Gott sei dank*" (thank God) and L stood for "*Liebe*" (dearest), always written before a family name. Her letters usually began with "I am well, G.S.D. How are L. Helmut and L. Eva?"

The New Apartment

A T LAST MY PARENTS passed their exams for medical licenses, and we moved to a large new apartment. My father looked so proud as he stood on the corner of Broadway and 111th Street and put up "M.D." shingles for himself and my mother. I couldn't quite remember seeing that expression on his face before, though maybe I had a long time ago. Counting back, I realized it had been five years since my parents had been able to work.

The new apartment was on the first floor of a thirteen-story building. There was a large waiting room and identical consulting room, and most fascinating, a room with medical equipment. As the medical supplies came in I begged for little bits of rubber tubing, bandages and test tubes for my "doctor kit" to use when my dolls got sick.

The day my mother brought me to visit the new apartment for the first time, she had been very excited. As we walked down the long corridor past the rooms where the patients were to come, she showed me the doorway to my room. It was full of light with a window to the street. Right in front of it, on the sidewalk, an organ grinder stood with his monkey, playing "La Marseillaise" — the French national anthem. That seemed like a good sign.

I had never had a room of my own before, and I knew I was supposed to be happy, planning where I would put things. Instead, I studied the door carefully. Did it have a lock? Was the lock strong enough to keep my brother out? Suddenly I felt very strange, as if I were two girls at once — one who had to worry about being safe in her new apartment, and another one who was watching her, realizing things weren't at all the way they should be.

The room turned out nicely after a new bed was moved in and shelves were put up for my dolls and a few games and books. It looked like a place where I could bring friends home when I went into third grade in my new school. Helmut liked his room, too, and busied himself making ship models and keeping up with books about the American and British navy's role in the war.

There were fewer reasons for my brother and I to fight now — but when we did, it was quite serious. One terrible time, my brother was chasing me and getting ready to give me a beating. I dashed into the bathroom for refuge. I was trying to close the hook-and-eye lock before he could get in the door but my pointer finger was caught in the lock, and he pushed the door so hard that it felt as if my finger was breaking. Hearing my screams, my mother rushed over and scolded my brother, and then examined my finger. "It'll be just fine," she said, putting a light bandage on it. But later, from the way it was healing, I still thought it was probably broken.

When my father saw his first patient the whole family was thrilled. A cook from the Chinese restaurant across Broadway from us had cut his hand, and his wife brought him in to have it stitched. The next day, he came back with his payment — a large bag of fortune cookies! He explained in his few English words that he had no money to pay. Too bad about that, but what a good omen! The cookies were our dessert for many days. Helmut and I giggled over the fortunes, made up new ones, and turned the cookies over and over to try to figure out how the little slips of paper got inside.

There were things that didn't work right in the new apartment — a window shade, a radiator and a sticky door. My father would call up the man who collected the rent and ask him to take a look. The man's answer was always the same: "Doctor, don't you know there's a war going on?" I understood he was trying to get out of fixing things, but still, it was a strange question, because there was never a minute that my parents didn't seem to have the war on their minds. They read the New York Times with great concern in the morning and listened to the radio news at night. I felt their worry and sadness deeply.

Hebrew School

MY CLASSMATES in fourth grade, Marilyn and the other Eva, both talked at once. "Come with us to Hebrew School after school! You'll really like it. They have good teachers, not like Miss M." None of us liked our fourth grade teacher, who was very strict and didn't make subjects interesting. She couldn't bend her knees when she walked and wasn't able to keep up with us in the schoolyard, so she just yelled a lot. I wasn't learning much.

That night, I asked my mother if I could walk to Temple Ansche Chesed on 100th Street with the girls after school tomorrow. She treated my request the same way as if I had asked to go to the park at Riverside Drive. "That sounds nice, dear."

The next day I visited the Hebrew class with my friends. The teacher read us a story about a funny little character named K'tonton and we played games with Hebrew letters. Then the rabbi came in and talked about a bible story in a dramatic way. This was a lot better than the dreary school hours at P.S. 165.

After supper, I tried out my carefully planned approach. It was best to get my father alone and ask him first. I described my visit, ending with "Papi, could I go to Hebrew school?" His answer was not a surprise. "I'm glad you want to learn about Judaism, but this costs money. You know we don't have any to spare!" "But Papi, how about talking with the rabbi? If you explained things, maybe he'd be willing to help."

It took a couple of days of discussions at home before the matter was settled. My mother made plenty of discouraging comments along the way. She preferred that Jewish customs were just carried out at home, and said that was sufficient. But now my father and I were on the streetcar after all, heading for the temple. Having him with me made this a very special occasion. After we arrived and my father went into the rabbi's office, one of my friends said, "Oh, you brought your grandfather." I tried to see Papi with her eyes. He had white hair, a high wrinkly forehead, and an anxious expression. Although I didn't like the remark, I could understand it. My father emerged from the meeting with a smile. "We worked it out — you can attend after school from now on," he said. "The rabbi is giving you a scholarship."

I learned to read Hebrew quickly, and my class began to translate the Torah. Over time, I began to get more involved, even attending the Junior Congregation services at the temple on some Saturday mornings.

The great thing about Hebrew School was that it made me feel good about being Jewish. This came just at a time when Life magazine, which I usually read in the waiting room after the patients had left, said that the war in Europe would be ending soon. I was beginning to feel less fear and more hope about the world.

When I suggested once that my mother come with me to the synagogue, it made her angry. "Why do you want to be so Jewish? What's wrong with you?" "But Mummy, you told me I should always be proud to be a Jew." "Well that doesn't mean you have to act like a *rebbitzin* (rabbi's wife)!" When I decided not to eat pork, according to the custom of more religious Jews, she conspired with my aunt to tell me that our dinners for special occasions consisted of roast beef — until I discovered it was really pork. She smiled at her own cleverness when I figured it out and confronted her.

I tried to comfort myself by adding this betrayal to my list of things I would never do to my children when I became a mother. I wished I could understand why my mother contradicted herself so often, on this matter of being Jewish as well as so many other things. One thing I did know was that her memories of poverty in the small towns in Poland where she lived as a child made her bitter. She often complained that her father (my grandfather), a rabbi who did social work in the Jewish community, barely supported her mother and her sisters. It helped a little to realize this wasn't just about me.

I liked sharing the joy or seriousness of Jewish holidays at the synagogue with the other kids. It was so different at home. When we observed the holidays, things were unbearably tense. It would start with my aunt being very nervous for the special food to be just right. Then my father would take out the Leica camera, a treasure that had somehow escaped from Vienna with us. He would start a long lecture instructing Helmut on how to take a picture, ordering him to hold it very carefully in order not to break it, since we didn't have money to fix it, and so on, and that was before my brother, already an expert photographer, could even touch the precious camera. Then my mother would attempt to supervise everything in her unique style of criticizing everyone — as if she was the *New York Times Book Review* and it was all a badly written book. Soon my brother would get very agitated, and one of his violent rages might follow. He would scream during a Seder, "There are bone splinters in the matzoh ball soup! Valli, you're trying to kill me!" Or "Mutti, You didn't light the Chanukah candles right! Do it over! Now!" I would count the hours until I could get out of the apartment again.

Becoming A Woman

MY MOTHER TOLD ME she had made a long trip to the live chicken market yesterday down in lower Manhattan. She had picked a chicken for them to butcher and brought it home on the subway. Now that it was Sunday, we would have the special time together that she had promised, when she would teach me things about how bodies work. She thought I should know more, now that I was ten.

She had explained how she learned anatomy and physiology with a cadaver in medical school years ago. Now she had figured out that you could get most of it straight from simply taking apart a chicken. After that, we would cook it! In these days, with World War II just ended, looking forward to a chicken dinner was special in itself.

During the week I yearned for more time with my mother, and today I was pleased to get her full attention. I usually saw Mutti for a few minutes between her visits with patients who had their appointments at our apartment, and then saw her again over a rushed dinner. Sundays were better — it was her day to cook dinner, while my Aunt Valli, who now ran the household, went off with her friends.

My mother and I sat at the red kitchen table opposite one another, staring at the chicken. It looked like others I had seen on a farm, except that it had no head. "First, we pluck the feathers out," Mother said. It was fun doing it together, until it got tiresome.

When we were finally done, she reached into the body cavity to take out various organs one at a time and explained their function. There was the liver, and the stomach, now seen in a new light.

"You see, *Nunilein*, I asked for a hen this time, so I could show you things about becoming a woman." My heart started racing and I wondered if I was blushing. Was this going to tie in with the little growing buds on my chest, which people seemed to stare at constantly, especially when I wore a sweater?

Slowly, she reached deeper into the hen and pulled out a long string with little round yellow things. "There, I've got it now. You see, every female is born with all the eggs she will ever need. In humans, one comes down the fallopian tube every month — it's regular, like the cycle of the moon. Isn't that a beautiful thing?" I nodded hard, relieved that this wasn't getting too personal.

"So these eggs need a blood supply when one of them is ready to grow into a baby. I'll tell you next Sunday what starts the egg growing — that's about the father. Anyway, every month the body is prepared just in case the egg will develop, and of course most of the time it doesn't. Take me, for example. I only had your brother Helmut and then later I had you. None of the rest of my eggs became babies."

She took a deep breath and continued. I could sense she had been planning this talk for a while, and was making a great effort to get it right. "So once a month the blood that isn't needed any more goes out of a woman's body. I think that will happen to you in a year or two, as it does with all girls. Then you will feel more connected to the earth, and we will be so proud and happy that you've become a woman!" She followed with necessary details, telling me how lucky I was that I wouldn't need to use rags to take care of this surplus blood, as she had in Poland, but could wear nice pillowy things called sanitary napkins.

Our talk was nearly over, and the chicken was placed into the pot with water, carrots, celery and paprika. I felt proud of my mother. She was so very smart, and also wise in the way that women just know things. I had heard other girls talk about how their mothers didn't explain their bodily changes at all, or expressed bad feelings on the subject. Although I often envied my friends whose moms seemed much more motherly, none of them could equal her in this moment.

As the soup simmered, a cozy fragrance was rising from the stove. And now my mother shared a secret for the first time. "You remember I told you how, back in Poland, I had to take care of my older sister Otti, the one who was mentally retarded. Well, she bled every month and I had to clean it up. I thought it was part of her handicap, so when it happened to me, I imagined I would become retarded, like her — or that maybe I was dying! No one told me what to expect until after my period started. So I swore when I had a daughter, I would help her understand beforehand!"

I was touched by her secret, and that she had thought of me as a person even before I existed. And I was looking forward to becoming a woman.

Friends

FRIENDS WERE EVERYTHING to me when I was ten. We could compare opinions, fix each other's hair, try out new board games, and play in the park at Riverside Drive together. When I visited the homes of my friends, I would watch their mothers very closely. What was it they did with their daughters, and how did they talk to them? I became quite attached to these moms, if they showed me attention and kindness.

Ora had long braids like mine, and she was smart and interesting. Her father was a professor at nearby Columbia University. My mother explained that he was very special, because he could read ancient Sanskrit and Egyptian hieroglyphics. Ora's mother had a pleasant way of talking with children, as if it was a grown-up conversation and children's comments were important. Sometimes I came along when Ora and her mom visited a gallery exhibit of one of Ora's painter uncles, Moses or Raphael Soyer. Or we would attend a concert of her uncle David Soyer, the cellist.

I tried out Mickel as a friend and walked home

from school with her many times. Her parents' apartment on 113th Street was nicer than ours, and her clothes looked newer. One day I picked up a penny on the street, a sign of good luck for me just like the four leaf clovers I searched for at Riverside Drive. She remarked, "The difference between you and me, is that you would bend over to pick up a penny, and I wouldn't." I never walked with her again.

My best friend by far was Moya. She had straight blonde hair and blue eyes that could look right through you. She had grown up in Burma with her younger sister Helga and small brother Tommy Tucker. What a lively bunch they were! Their Irish father had worked for the British government in Burma and had died there. Their mother, Carola, then brought them to New York. She was from Germany, but was strongly anti-Nazi. We girls used to follow strangers down Broadway, playing detective as we looked for clues to whatever mysterious business they might be undertaking that day. At our homes, we created complicated plays complete with costumes and put them on for our families. Like me, Moya was always ready to have an adventure, whether it was in the park or just in our imaginations.

Moya's mother Carola, still a grieving widow, often took me into her confidence. At times she was overwhelmed by the chaos of New York life. When the three children quarreled — which was inevitable because of their strong personalities — she was beside herself. At one time, when they were fighting and calling her too often at work, she was so upset that she decided to place them in a *Kinderheim* and take a break. I hated the idea that there could be an orphanage, even in New York, for children who actually had a parent. Knowing that I missed them terribly, Carola took me along when she fetched them a few weeks later. On the long train ride, I had vivid and painful memories of the train in Switzerland that took me to visit my brother at his *Kinderheim*. Would Moya be crying when we arrived, as Helmut always did when we visited? No such thing! She was playing cheerfully, and just dashed into her mother's arms. Watching them, I thought about my own mother who was obviously overwhelmed at times, too. I felt grateful that I had my aunt as a kind of second mother to me.

Rose Anne was a friend I met at summer camp. I had picked out Camp Woodland from the ads in the back of the *New York Times* magazine section that spring. The camp advertised cultural activities, folk music and nature study. It sounded different from the other camps I had been to since I was seven. Competition in sports at those camps always made me miserable. Since I usually just flinched when a ball was flying towards me, I was picked last in any sport. I persuaded my father to talk with the director of Camp Woodland, and my parents agreed to let me go there.

It turned out that our folk song leader was the great Pete Seeger! My counselor Sophie was from Providence and knew my relatives there. From the start, I felt I belonged. And from the first day in our cabin of ten-year-old girls, I liked Rose Anne. She wasn't homesick or spoiled, like some of the other girls. She could talk about any subject, and it seemed as if we had an eight-week conversation during that happy summer. Rose Anne complained to me that she thought she was a follower instead of a leader, but I didn't find any fault with that.

Later, during the school year, I visited her in the Bronx, where we enjoyed roller-skating or riding a tandem bike around the nearby reservoir, always keeping our conversation going. Her father was an activist lawyer, and he and her mom felt deeply for people who had suffered anywhere in the world. I never talked about my life in Europe, but Rose Anne's parents somehow sensed something about it.

I was an American girl now, almost completely. Having the freedom of the streets and subways usually felt good to me. It meant meeting a rough situation once in a while, and I had to develop "street smarts." In New York City there's a lot to watch out for, with gangs about and weird men on the prowl. Most often I was out with a friend, and we provided some protection for one another.

Mother's Day

IT WAS NOW my mother's custom to treat Mother's Day as a day of mourning. At breakfast, she would stretch her forearm across her forehead with her elbow jutting out, in her headache position. "I hope you didn't get me any presents or cards," she would begin. "I'm sorry I ever became a mother."

My brother would look as though he had been punched in the stomach. I knew that her words were aimed more at him than at me. It was her way of punishing him for being crazy, for behaving badly when his delusions got very strong, for not being the adorable smiling boy dressed in *lederhosen* any more.

As for me, I didn't show her how I felt, because it only encouraged her to carry on further. I'm not sure I even showed myself how I felt. I believed that I, too, was being punished by her words. I was somehow disappointing. Was it for failing to fix my brother, or for refusing to follow some of my mother's orders — or other reasons?

When Helmut showed signs of becoming agitated, my mother would turn to me and say, "Please, Eva, you're the only one who can talk to him. See if you can make him stop!" I would try, and sometimes it worked, but not always. When he was on the rampage, he would hit my mother, father, or aunt. None of them had the slightest idea of how to control my brother's behavior, despite the professional training my parents had received. The women screamed, and my father retreated. Then Helmut would clomp away to his room, his heavy footsteps echoing through the apartment, and slam his door.

With me, it would start as a brother and sister fight, but the beatings would go beyond that. He was tall, strong and muscular. I learned to avoid fighting back because it only increased his rage. The force of his punches often made bruises that changed colors the next day. I would look at my bruised arm or face in the mirror, and blush with shame. I came from a bad family that had a secret!

I would study the angle of impact, and figure out a believable story to tell when people asked "What happened?" "Oh, I fell when I was roller-skating in the park," I might say. My mother had warned me often that I mustn't say anything to harm her reputation, which she depended on to make a living. I didn't even dare to imagine what would happen if I ever told.

Around this time, I switched over from calling my mother "Mummy" to calling her "Mother." She considered this lack of endearment cold and hostile. Maybe it was, yet I loved her very much. The longing was always there, for her smile, her wise words, the rare special moments of fun together.

"What's wrong with you, always going off somewhere instead of staying home?" she would ask me resentfully. I wasn't afraid to say what I thought any more. "It's not a home, Mother. A home is a place that's private, but I live at your offices and I'm supposed to keep still and stay out of the way of your patients. A home is a place that's safe, but here, it's dangerous, with Helmut acting violent." She would respond angrily: "You are so ungrateful for the advantages I've given you!"

I started begging to be sent away from New York City to live with one of the two cousin families in Providence, Rhode Island. I seldom saw them, but loved them dearly. Mother would say, "Ha, so you think you'd like to be with your Aunt 'Carnation'!"

My aunt's name was Rose. "She does nothing all day but swoon and complain! Anyway, what makes you think she'd want you?" In fact, I had enjoyed her hospitality on my infrequent visits. Or, "You can't stay with your Aunt Elsie — she is weird! She puts a kerchief on her head to open the refrigerator door!" The second part was true, as she had special rules of her own for handling her arthritis. The important thing was, she and my uncle were affectionate and supportive towards me. At any rate, I had to give up on going to live with relatives. Maybe there was another way for me to leave.

New Worlds Open To Me

I SAT DOWN IN the cafeteria at Hunter College Junior High School. It was nearly spring, and I was beginning to feel settled in my new school. At first the loud voices of the girls at lunchtime, with their tone of near hysteria had gotten on my nerves, but it didn't matter so much now. Two new friends, Joyce and Maria, would be joining me any minute, and at last I had something to belong to — our little threesome. We weren't always together in classes, but it was more important to me to have friends to sit with at lunch.

The idea of my coming to this school started last year when my sixth grade teacher, Miss Kennedy, invited me to her house while she was home on medical leave. She told me "I really think you're dying at school. I want you to take the test for Hunter to get out of the neighborhood, and learn with other bright girls." She knew that I was fearful of going to the girl's bathroom because of roaming bands of eighth grade boys who harassed us on the way, even with sexual threats. And she knew I wasn't learning enough at P.S. 169 to feel challenged. When I passed the Hunter entrance exam, I called her at her home. Her interest and encouragement touched me deeply, especially coming while she was in treatment for cancer.

At first I had a rough start at the school. I was shy, especially if I was having a bad week at home. My big question was, whom would I hang out with? The rich girls who lived on the East Side near the school were too interested in their cashmere sweaters; the nice Jewish girls from the Bronx had been very protected and I felt much older than them; the girls who seemed to have read every novel under the sun, and could criticize them all, were too intimidating. I knew I could have a good personality, if someone would just accept me first. But I must have looked like a dull mouse and I seemed to attract awkward loners. When I talked with my mother about not being popular, she was surprisingly sympathetic. She reminded me that I would get stronger in this new situation, and that I should give other girls more of a chance to know me.

My confidence increased, and then I met Joyce and Maria, both of whom had previously been at a school for "professional children." Joyce had been a child actress, and was once in a play with Marlon Brando, whom she still had a crush on. She had straight blonde hair and wore her skirts straight, not slightly askew like mine. Maria, the dark-haired daughter of a Russian mother, had enthusiasm for anything to do with the arts, and was a pianist of great skill. Both had given up performing for the rigors of Hunter Junior High homework.

After school we three often took long walks on Riverside Drive, with many giggles. Once in a while we took a bus to radio station WNYC on a late Saturday afternoon to be in the audience of the *Oscar Brand Show*, where we could watch live folk music performances. On Sunday, if the weather was mild, we went to Greenwich Village together to listen and join in with young folk singers playing the guitar at Washington Square.

Joyce was on a radio show on Saturday mornings called *Young Book Reviewers on the Air*. When she invited me to join her, I found I was less shy in front of a microphone than in person. The most interesting show was one where we talked with Jackie

Robinson about his new book about becoming the first Negro major league baseball player. (Yes, we said "Negro" in those days.)

YOUNG BOOK REVIEWERS ON THE AIR

New worlds were opening for me. I realized that by doing exciting things away from home, I could have some control over my life. It was easier to forget about the terror in the house. I went home to my room mainly for homework and sleep, and only joined my family for meals.

I secretly yearned for time alone with each of my parents. Occasionally my mother took me shopping for clothes, or my father went to the park or museum with me. Most of the time they were quite preoccupied with studying psychoanalysis, their new specialty in medicine. They were each being analyzed themselves, but my father wouldn't admit it. When I asked him where he was going, knowing from my mother that he had an appointment with his analyst, he would just say "Stop." So I would tell Aunt Valli, "Daddy's gone to see Dr. Stop."

It seemed to me that my parents were aiming toward more wisdom and self-understanding, which I respected. The trouble was, they were not making a better family life. They were constantly afraid of my brother, now that he was seventeen and even stronger. As for me, I went into a sort of trance when his terrifying outbursts of screaming and hitting would start. It was as if my mind went outside my body. That way I felt safer while I waited for it to be over.

Today in the school lunchroom, Maria and Joyce plopped down in the chairs I'd saved for them and ate their sandwiches. Maria showed us poems she had written and illustrated, and Joyce had us laughing like crazy about a funny thing that happened on stage in one of her Broadway plays. I did a satirical skit for them, imitating one of my teachers. And then we gathered up our schoolbooks and went to our next classes.

Puzzling Over
Contradictions

WHEN I CAME HOME from summer camp, my parents had moved to a large apartment on 5th Avenue. The idea started last year, when my mother quoted a patient as saying, "Doctor, I'm tired of coming to the slums to see you!" I knew my mother was very eager to get out of the old neighborhood after that, but I was still surprised to learn of the move when she wrote me at camp. My brother was doing somewhat better at this time. He was traveling with Ernst Papanek, a youth group leader we had known in Vienna, so he was out of my parents' way for the summer.

My mother's new office was elegant, with ultramodern furniture, including an amoeba-shaped desk and an uncomfortable couch. She was becoming well-known in the psychoanalytic world now, training other analysts and giving popular lectures. Her appointment book was full. I was glad she felt so much pride in her work and the apartment.

My father's office contained his huge book collection and some Viennese memorabilia. It also had a psychoanalytic couch, but this one was just right, not too hard. The room was filled with bookcases and served as a kind of retreat for him. Between sessions he was often lying on his couch reading a novel or a medical journal.

The family bedrooms were in a separate wing. There was one main door to the apartment, and it certainly felt as if life was centered around the patients. For dinner, Aunt Valli would serve us soup in the kitchen at 4:50 after my mother's four o'clock patient, followed by the main course at 5:50 after the next patient, with tea and dessert when the seven o'clock patient was gone. Only by eight o'clock did the waiting room become a living room. If I was done with my homework by then, I could go there to read magazines or listen to music on the record player.

On afternoons when I had friends visiting in my room, Mother would pop in for a few minutes and participate. If we were talking about James Joyce, she would have an insightful comment. If we were discussing politics, she was up on the latest news about the issue. Of course my friends found her fascinating and even wished their moms had her charm and knowledge.

The amazing thing was that so many of the things Mother said in private to us, her own family, were disparaging. Aunt Valli hadn't cooked the dinner right. My father didn't see enough patients today to make a decent living. My brother behaved like a terrorist or a Nazi. And I, her daughter, wasn't wearing the right clothes or makeup to look like much — and my activities away from home were unnecessary and foolish. We all waited for the good moments when she showed affection and even compassion. My father lived for those special times when she would bestow her love on him. We each looked up to her very much. How was it possible that she could so embitter the daily life of the family?

It was hard to understand what my mother wanted from me since she was so often displeased. When I thought about it I came up with just a few points. Like many mothers who had lived in a Germanic culture, she expected total adherence to her ideas and obedience to her orders. Except, we were in America now! She also wanted my adoration, like an enthusiastic fan in her audience. But I wanted a mother, not a diva. And then, she wanted me to be successful and beautiful, in order to reflect well on her — but not so much that I'd upstage her. In her best moments, she just wanted to give and take attention and love, which was what I wanted, too.

My father and I got along wonderfully when we were alone. If he was free when I got home from school, I would go to his office to chat. He loved hearing about my school, friends, activities or opinions. Sometimes I could see that he was depressed, but it made me happy that he could enjoy me and feel better.

Another strange contradiction: the connection

between my father and me disappeared as soon as my mother was in the same room with us. No matter how negative or irrational my mother was, my father never disagreed with her in my presence. Nor did he intervene when my brother hit me, except for a mild comment that he should stop. At those times I didn't feel he was acting like a father. Wasn't it his job to protect me?

My brother had especially paradoxical qualities. He was getting good grades in college and it was obvious that he was incredibly smart. He could help me do an advanced math problem or answer a tough question. "Helmut, what is philosophy?" "Well, Nuni, it's the truth about the truth. You see, people have been trying to figure out the meaning of life for centuries..." He enjoyed explaining Austrian history to me, and we often sang songs in several languages together or created comic poems. He composed one in German when our mother gave one of her famous European-style soirées. A rough translation:

While the guests are feasting,
Their buttons nearly bursting,
It's just leftovers for the kid,
And now the liquor has been hid!

The trouble was that, at any moment, my brother could suddenly be overtaken with his delusional ideas, fears and rages. I watched him very closely so that I could notice a mood change early on. Maybe I could walk away or perhaps talk him out of it. It was exhausting for me. I had once met his psychiatrist and considered him to be just one more ineffective adult. When would my parents find any treatments for my brother that would actually do some good? Why were they, such outstanding doctors, mental health experts, as helpless as the most ignorant parents when it came to my brother?

I didn't dare to ask these questions out loud. I could only guess the reasons. My father believed that he had been a poor parent and had partly caused my brother's mental illness. He seemed to be lost in sorrow and guilt about it. My mother felt guilty for having placed my brother in the orphanage in Switzerland, and may have promised herself that she would never send him away again.

I was coming to believe that my family members were broken inside through the terror we experienced in Austria under the Nazis, and the stress of the refugee years. I was determined not to let that happen to me. I had my own feelings of fear and sadness but I refused to give in to them. It still seemed possible to me that I could have a new life when I left home. I figured I'd better keep myself in good shape for it!

I often thought about how I would do things differently when I had children some day. I would give them my full love and attention, with plenty of time for shared activities. My work would be set up to fit with my family life, not the other way around. I would protect and guide my children. And their father would be active with them as well.

Changing Schools

IN THE NINTH GRADE, while taking advanced German, I was tracked with a group of German girls from the Yorkville neighborhood who talked about nothing but their church and the German cultural events in which their families were involved. I was uncomfortable around them, wondering if their fathers had been Nazis. The school atmosphere of intense competition at Hunter was beginning to bother me as well. One day near the end of the first term of ninth grade, I hatched a plan. Why not try to transfer to Bronx High School of Science, another special public school for New York students who could do advanced work? It was rumored to have a good atmosphere. Besides, unlike Hunter — which had only girls and female teachers — it was co-educational.

At lunchtime, I suggested to Joyce and Maria that we all ditch school the next day and take two subways to the Bronx to see if we could transfer. Joyce demurred, saying her mother would kill her if she played hooky. But Maria, who was not as closely watched at home, excitedly agreed.

The next day we showed up at Bronx Science. In a bold mood, I asked if we could see the principal. As soon as we were seated in Dr. Meister's office, he asked, "Where are your parents?" Almost in one voice, Maria and I said, "They're always working, they can't come." Fortunately, he heard me out as I described our dissatisfactions with Hunter and our yearning for more science classes — rather an exaggeration — not mentioning the part about meeting boys. "But you haven't taken the test for this school," he argued. I said, "The Hunter test is just as hard, maybe harder, and we passed that!"

"All right, let's try it." the principal finally said. "Just bring in your parents first." Maria and I looked at each other as she rolled her eyes and I raised my eyebrows. She probably thought what I did: "That'll be the day!" Then I went home and started talking with my father about it, and he finally agreed to "give up an afternoon" and go up to the Bronx to talk with Dr. Meister for both me and Maria. We were accepted, and started school there mid-year.

It turned out that we had made a good choice. At Bronx Science, the emphasis was more on the pleasure and practicality of learning than on competition. Our programs included many science labs, nature field trips to local parks, and even shop classes. The school had only started accepting girls two or three years earlier and I was happy to see that we were on a completely equal footing with the boys.

My male friends gave me extra help with physics and chemistry, which I needed badly, and took me to a dance once in a while. Maria and I sensed that we weren't ready for boyfriends yet, but we learned to be at ease with the guys at school.

It felt great to have chosen my own path. I felt a lot of gratitude to be in America, a place where your fate was not all laid out for you, where you could make choices. And maybe I was lucky after all, that my parents mostly left me to my own devices.

Decisions in the Dark
Age 14

WHAT A WONDERFUL invitation! My dad told me he felt I was mature enough to go to the opera and he would be getting tickets soon! Mother couldn't come because she was writing an important lecture. We would be seeing *La Bohème* on a Sunday afternoon. I knew some of the arias because Papi was in the habit of whistling or humming operas, especially when he was shaving. He told me the story of *La Bohème* and it just fit in with my fascination for the artists I observed on my treks to Greenwich Village.

When he came home with the tickets, Papi mentioned that Helmut would be coming, too. I felt my stomach falling towards my feet. I knew how likely it was that my brother would get agitated and break out into a tantrum or worse. He could turn into a terrifying bully at any time.

At last it was the big day. When the three of us arrived at the Metropolitan Opera House, the usher showed us into box seats. I was surprised at the luxurious seats — like other refugee families we knew, my parents hardly ever splurged. I felt like

a very special daughter. The dresses of the ladies sitting nearby were beautiful, and I liked the smell of perfumes mixed with dust. When the velvet curtains went up, I was entranced. All my senses were wide open as I watched Mimi move gracefully about the stage and listened to the music. I was thinking happily, "I'm getting back a part of the Viennese life I would have had — I'm an opera-goer now."

Suddenly my brother was dissatisfied with something and poked me sharply with his elbow. After situations like this, I never could remember how it started, because it was something so small. Did it irritate him that I tapped my foot, or rattled my program? He was whispering to me in his harshest German, and finally punched me hard in the stomach. I lost my breath and my stomach hurt badly. I'm not sure what kept me from telling my father — maybe I just thought he wouldn't know what to do.

Tears rolled off my face for a very long time as the music went on. My thoughts were racing. This wasn't fair — this wasn't a way I could live my life! I was so attuned to the opera that I hadn't gotten out of my body the way I usually managed when my brother attacked me. I was as helpless now as I had been when I was five on the ship to America and he had thrown that shoe at my face.

What to do, what to do...Okay, there were two things I *could* do. I would leave home as soon as possible, definitely earlier than at eighteen. Since my mother could not bring herself to send my brother to a treatment program away from home, I figured this was the only way I could be safe.

The other thing I would do was to become a psychologist someday. In my work, I wouldn't just help each person have more self-understanding or feel a little better, like the psychoanalysts who treated each of my family members. Surely I could find a way to work with whole families to solve problems. I was already learning psychology anyway. I'd read some of the books on my parents' shelves, and had been overhearing case discussions and editing my parents' lectures for a couple of years.

At intermission I dashed to the ladies room and splashed cold water on my face. When I returned, I didn't cry again until Mimi died onstage. I didn't reveal the decisions I had made in the dark that day to anyone, but I knew they were absolutely firm.

Leaving My Family

ALTHOUGH I WAS a good student, toward the end of my sophomore year I began to realize there was no way I could pass the required New York State Regents exams that were coming up in the spring. I was nervous and exhausted, since my brother often forced the whole family to stay up long after midnight. He would hold fierce interrogations in the kitchen as if we were prisoners of war suspected of colluding with the enemies that he believed were chasing us.

His voice full of rage, Helmut would ask: "Mutti, how dare you call up the Podvolny's, those damn Communists!" She would answer, "But they're Russian emigres, Helmut, and they were good to us when we first came to America." Or, "Aunt Valli, just what did you have in mind, going to the German butcher shop in Yorkville last week? You should know they are Nazis plotting to come after us!" Our aunt responded mildly, "Helmi, dear, I only went there because they have your favorite kind of *wurst*."

Sooner or later I would get a headache from the tension and the bright light. As his ranting continued on, louder and louder, my heart was usually racing. I knew his fists might fly at any moment if he didn't get the answers he wanted. I figured he was re-playing the day when the Nazis tortured him in the Austrian jail so many years ago, only this time he was the torturer. Sometimes I tried to soothe him. Mostly I just tried to imagine I was somewhere else, and let myself go partly limp or partly numb inside.

I decided to confront my mother in her office between patients. "I'm going to flunk school this term," I told her. This could get her attention more fully than if I said that I was unhappy. "Helmut is much worse, and you still haven't sent him to a hospital, where he belongs! At least let me go somewhere else so I can cram for my tests!" This time she heard my plea. She arranged for me to spend the last two weeks of the term with an elderly refugee colleague, Emmy.

I took a crosstown bus ride through Central Park to Emmy's office and apartment on the West Side. The quiet of my room there was heaven. At the end of her workday, Emmy listened to Beethoven records and cooked delicious German food. Over a relaxing dinner, she asked eagerly for details about how my day had gone. If only I could stay for the rest of high school! But when I raised the question on the phone with my mother, she said Emmy was too old to keep a teenager. The day I left Emmy's apartment with my small suitcase, there were tears in my eyes. As always, the crosstown bus placed me right in front of the apartment building where my family lived. But I certainly didn't call it "my home."

It was the end of June and I had just enough time to pack for summer camp. My brother and I more or less ignored each other. Before I left, I learned I had gotten A's on my Regents exams. What a relief! This raised my grades that had gotten dangerously low in several subjects. With the chaos going on in the house, there had been many days when I couldn't concentrate.

The eight weeks away at camp gave me a marvelous escape into a community of teenagers. The camp was at an old Shaker village in Massachusetts. We were asked to choose between various work projects that would restore the village to the condition it was in when the Shakers were thriving there. We had a kind of student government, and my friends voted me in as mayor for a two-week term. There were many wonderful trips to nearby concerts at Tanglewood and dance recitals at a place called Jacob's Pillow. We had our own creative activities as well. My favorite was singing in the chorus, where I was the only girl in the tenor section. The music counselor, Hal, would point in our direction and say "Men — and Eva — let's try that passage again".

At first, that summer, I let myself almost forget about my family and got absorbed into the activities and friendships at camp. But by August I began to feel anxious, and I knew I needed a plan. I sat under a favorite tree alone and thought about my possibilities. If only I could tell someone! Well, if anyone could keep a secret I supposed it was Hal. I would break my mother's rule of silence and tell him that my brother was beating me, and I needed to live elsewhere. Perhaps I could live with him and his wife and help with their young children — or perhaps among his wide circle of musician friends there was another family that could use a mother's helper. I even told him I was good with children, an unproven boast.

Just as I'd hoped, Hal took me seriously. His apartment wasn't large enough for me to live there, he explained, but he thanked me for the offer and promised to do a search for me when we each got back to New York.

After I returned from camp, my parents, who had genuinely missed me, seemed to be puzzled by my detached air. I gave no explanation. A week later Hal called to tell me he had made several inquiries, but no one wanted to take in a girl under sixteen.

The next week, I witnessed a horrific midnight scene in which my brother threatened my father with such vehemence that I was afraid for Papi's life. Just as I was considering calling the police myself, the crisis was suddenly over. The next morning Helmut picked up his briefcase and went off to his class at NYU as if nothing had happened. I warned my father that if he had the bad judgment to keep my brother at home, this was the last time he would see me. Even as I used strong words, not knowing how I would carry out my threat, I was aware that my parents still couldn't bear the thought of a locked psychiatric ward for their son.

That afternoon I had an appointment with a psychoanalyst I had been seeing for half a year. Until then I had hidden most of the violence from Joan, my therapist. I was not really comfortable with her because my mother, a senior analyst, made important decisions about junior analysts like Joan who were in the same psychoanalytic institute. But now I just had to describe the chaotic scene from yesterday. As she listened, a tear rolled down her cheek. I was very moved by her reaction. She promised to take some action, though I doubted that she could influence my mother.

Joan conferred with Emmy and then my parents, who finally did consent to my departure. By the end of that week I was living on the West Side again. The arrangement was made with a couple whose mentally ill daughter had been a patient of Emmy's. The room I was to live in was still stuffed with the daughter's clothes and knick-knacks while she was in the hospital, which gave me an eerie feeling. I didn't want this couple to act like parents towards me. They were not too interested in me, either. I was simply a lodger whose parents paid my board. My new life brought out a kind of cheerful bravado while I lived on my own like a college girl in my junior year of high school.

I had promised my mother not to tell anyone that I lived away from home, except for two friends who each had somewhat irregular family situations themselves. One was Ellen, a girlfriend from camp who lived nearby. The other was George, my old nursery school chum from Switzerland. He was now attending a Yeshiva high school (a Jewish school) in New York, and we went on dates to one of his basketball games or a movie every week. He ended each date with a few shy kisses. His companionship helped me regain my balance.

When I wanted to see my other friends, I would suggest we meet at their homes or in a museum, not giving my new address. I kept in touch with my parents by calling from my school's public telephone at certain times of day when I knew my brother would not be home. Once, I was sent to the vice principal for using the phone without a hall pass. I was frightened to be in trouble. I decided to risk revealing that I lived away from home, and why. To my surprise, the vice principal was sympathetic. He gave me a note permitting me to use the phone at any time. Best of all, he agreed not to call my mother, who would have been livid if she thought I had revealed a family secret.

Kentucky Summer

A LITTLE BEFORE SUMMER, my brother became so violent against our mild-mannered father that my parents were finally ready to have him hospitalized. He was to undergo lengthy treatment at a private psychiatric hospital in upstate New York. My parents directed me to return home immediately to live with them again. When I did, I found a dreadful gloom was filling the household. I think the grief my parents showed came from their long delayed recognition of how serious my brother's problems were, and their inability to help him. My own sadness was about his stolen childhood, and to some extent, my own. And now Helmut was a young adult who had lost his freedom and had to live among difficult strangers, which must have terrified him.

The city was hot and muggy. As usual, it was up to me to plan something to do for the summer — and I was eager to leave the heaviness in the house. My work project at the Shaker village for the last summer had gone well. But now I wanted to start helping people living in poverty — maybe that would become a part of my life's work.

My friend Rose Anne had told me about her excellent summer at a volunteer work camp in Pennsylvania last year. I took her advice to contact the American Friends Service Committee and they accepted me as a volunteer. Soon after school ended, I was waving goodbye to my father and boarding a Greyhound bus leaving New York City for a Quaker project. My destination: Harlan County, Kentucky to work at Pine Mountain Settlement School.

The closer the bus came to my stop, the hotter and dustier I felt. By the time I got there, I thought I didn't smell very good, but the camp counselor who met my bus seemed glad to see me. As we began to drive up the long mountain road in a pickup truck, she warned me that it was quite bumpy and that there were twenty hairpin turns up to the top of Pine Mountain. I stifled my fear by imagining the motion of the truck was just like a lurching subway. The counselor continued: these local teenagers really needed our help. They lived in remote areas, and had to walk a long way to get to their school. We were going to work together with them on our summer construction and farming projects. I could count on having fun, too, as we'd include them in games, swimming and so on.

I settled into a shared room and was toured around the school buildings and small farm by early arrivers, mostly New York kids. Everything about Pine Mountain pleased me — the smell of the grass, the small starts of planted vegetables, the hand-built farm structures, even remembrances of the children's schoolwork in the empty classrooms. And I had never heard such beautiful bird songs.

The next morning, we had group meditation in the Quaker manner. I allowed myself to think of my family, giving a silent prayer for my brother and hoping that my parents and aunt were recovering from the shock of his hospitalization.

Afterwards Sandy, our director, began a meeting to lay out plans for the summer. We would build a large toolshed for the farm, and help with the harvesting at the end of summer. And now he had a difficult decision to put on the agenda. A Negro boy from Pittsburgh, an outstanding student named Syl who had some ties with the Quakers, had volunteered to join us. Including him was risky because of the intense racial prejudice of Southerners and their harsh "Jim Crow" segregation system.

There was danger for him and for the rest of us as well. We voted by voice, and I think it was unanimous that we wanted him to come. Each of us had felt miserable on the way to Pine Mountain when we saw signs for separate "White" and "Colored" restrooms and water fountains. Here was a chance to show that people could live in harmony instead of this hatred!

A couple of days later, the pickup truck was sent down the mountain to pick up Syl from the bus station. We waited tensely before dinner, and suddenly he was there, stepping out of the truck with a crooked smile. As he walked toward us swinging his suitcase, showing energy and confidence, we felt sure we'd made the right decision.

A handful of kids from the surrounding areas came to work with the twenty of us volunteers from up north. But socializing afterwards was difficult at first. "Hey, we're getting up a baseball game later. Wanna join us?" one of our group would say. "I ain't playing no game with that nigger!" "Oh, come on, he's our pitcher — and we really need you for first base." Or, "I hope you're coming to the party tonight. Your friend R.B. is going to bring his guitar and teach us some more folk songs." "No, my daddy says I can't come to a party where there's a nigger." We slowly brought some of them around, with friendliness and social pressure and inviting their parents to visit.

It was different with their older brothers. Now and then, a few came over in an old car and harassed us. One of them leaned out the car window and yelled, "Y'know, they used to shoot union organizers that came from up north, around here. Just so's you know..." The young men should have had jobs, but there were none around. It came to me that they were just the type who would have been Nazi recruits in Europe a dozen years ago. Once, I was sitting under a tree with a young man who'd come to fetch his younger sister. "This is a cottonwood tree," he said. I thought it was just a friendly remark. "That's the kind they use to hang niggers" came next. Somehow our group leaders protected us from the local thugs and made sure we each had a good experience.

I had become close friends with Syl. There was a wave of understanding between us from the start. It was as if he already knew that I was used to dealing with violent threats, and I surely knew how it felt to act brave on the outside and feel scared on the inside. We would talk late into the night about what it was like for him to grow up as a son of divorced parents, and the quiet rage he felt when he saw black women being taken advantage of in his hometown near Pittsburgh. I told him how my family's wartime experiences had broken my brother's health and how, back in New York, we were hardly a family any more.

Of course, I was falling in love with Syl that summer — but there was no direction for us to grow. He lived in a faraway city and we would probably not be attending college near each other. Besides, I couldn't bear to add to my parents' stress right now by bringing home a young man who wasn't Jewish, let alone of a different race.

At the end of summer, we had a great celebration of the completion of our work. I now knew how to build a stone wall, raise a wooden building, tend crops, and cook for a large group. I must have learned dozens of Kentucky folk songs and English country dances that had been handed down from the first British immigrants in Appalachia. In many ways I was stronger now than when I had arrived.

Traveling home alone on the bus, I cried quietly just as I had in earlier years when a summer camp ended. This time there was a separation that affected my heart...

When I got home, I enjoyed telling stories of the summer to my family, carefully leaving out details that would have upset them. My mother could sense my sudden loneliness, and decided to let me get a kitten. I called her Pretty Saro, after my favorite Kentucky song.

My mood was also lifted by an unexpected letter from Antioch College that had arrived at the house before I did. It said that a Quaker couple who visited the summer project had suggested that I was just the kind of student their college wanted! The school required three years of intensive study, interspersed with two years of a variety of co-op jobs or internships. Through these job placements, one could get a head start on choosing and even learning a career. It felt as though an invisible force was guiding me! An application for Antioch was included, and I filled it out before my senior year at high school started.

Starting College

Yellow Springs, Ohio — 1952

A s the overnight train chugged toward Ohio, I clutched my acceptance letter for Antioch College along with a welcome letter that said anything freshmen forgot to bring could be found at the bookstore. This led to a hilarious conversation between me and my mother about what that "anything" might be. I could hardly believe we were chatting congenially in a "roomette" on the train. Mother herself had suggested that she drop me off at college. It was our first trip together outside of New York City that was longer than a weekend.

For most of the year, my mother had been deriding me for giving up a scholarship to a New York State university, which I'd won through an exam. I knew that money wasn't the issue. She just didn't want to separate from me again. While on the elevator in our building, she had even said to a colleague, "Eva's running away from home at seventeen" — actually leaving out the part about my going to college! More recently she had resigned herself to the fact that "Eva's going out west to Ohio." (As sophisticated as Mother was, sometimes she sounded like a greenhorn who just got off the boat.)

Now a porter had come to make up our beds in the roomette. As we rode along I felt contented and safe, with the train rocking us both to sleep.

We arrived in Yellow Springs the next morning, found my dormitory, and met my very friendly roommate Shirley, a girl from Ohio. My mother helped me settle in, and we parted on affectionate terms. Finally alone for a while, I sat down on my bed and reviewed the long list of goals I had for this first year. I wanted to make new friends in my dormitory. I also planned to spend time in town, meeting American families and learning more about how they lived and raised their children. I would try to get my required courses out of the way fast, so I could concentrate on sociology and psychology sooner. I hoped to meet boys for long deep conversations — and to go to dances. And I wanted to join activist groups that were against the Korean War and the social inequities on the home front.

Many of my goals materialized almost right away. I was lucky to meet a senior named Bud who explained how, with my background, I could take exams to get out of many of the required freshman classes. Antioch required that I receive "work credits" every year, and my first job was assisting in a nursery school on campus. I also babysat for some of my professors to earn movie money, and it was fun to get to know their families. Meanwhile the junior and senior men seemed to be swarming around the freshman girls, and most of us had about as many dates as we could find time for, without getting "serious."

C. S.

The Fire On Campus

In February, 1953 there was a fire in my dormitory at Antioch College. Thankfully, there were no injuries or lives lost. Here's what I wrote to my family at that time:

Dear Family,

I'll tell you how the whole fire came about. It started in the attic. I smelled smoke myself for half an hour but didn't think much about it. When I heard the alarm go off at 7 p.m. my first thought was to save my blue coat and my life! I ran out while the others groaned, thinking it was a fire drill, but I knew it was the real thing (and told them to get out too). I live on the third floor, the fire was on the fifth, so we started a line of people to hand things out of the building: firemen inside, kids outside. Much of my stuff was taken out: my guitar, typewriter and records. (The reason) I called Daddy up in tears (was) because I was afraid I'd never see the rest of my things.

Of course we couldn't return to the dorm. We slept in the gym the first night. It brought back many memories to be a refugee again, but it's easier the second time. Some of the girls suffered severe emotional upset, but I didn't do too badly. I'm used to moving around, making the best of a bad situation!

I am fine now, settled in a neat, large, light, friendly room in town. Last night I went out on a date and when I came back my roommates Fritzie and Jackie had put together my broken phonograph and were playing a record to surprise me!

Forty girls lost everything they owned. I am missing all of my luggage and my summer dresses. All else is either found or of insignificant value. This is most unusually good luck. By all means don't worry.

Love,

Eva

P.S. I was in yesterday's newspaper, am sending clipping.

The picture shows me laughing amidst the wet and smoky remains of my dormitory room. "It's only stuff!"

The Student Peace Club

I had been thinking for a while about the origins of World War II, and how it could have been prevented, or possibly shortened, by a more politically conscious public. Hitler could have been stopped in Germany in the early 1930s if enough people had paid attention and seen through his ugly hate propaganda. And now America was getting involved in a war in Korea that I considered counterproductive. I didn't want to be a passive bystander, as so many Germans had been back then. It seemed completely natural for me to join the newly forming Student Peace Club. I couldn't have imagined that this would later result in the most difficult part of my freshman year.

I was eager to attend the first club meeting in the fall. I spoke up about my hopes that America's policy would change, resulting in a peaceful settlement of the Korean conflict. It was a surprise to me when my earnest speech got me elected president, but I accepted — despite misgivings about the possible time commitment involved. I suggested a program of inviting speakers from a number of different political groups to a series of meetings to discuss alternatives to the war. The group quickly agreed. We would not be able to vote until we were twenty-one, but we could educate our fellow students all the same.

One of our members was a Quaker named Hank who had lunch with me from time to time to talk about politics and his intentions to become a conscientious objector. I liked his smile and his good ideas. In the spring, I complained to him that a guest speaker from a left-wing political group had sent me a stack of their newsletters in advance, asking me to distribute them. What *chutzpah* (nerve)! We had no intention of promoting his organization, just finding out their point of view.

Two weeks later, I was in my physical education class in my skimpy gym suit, doing exercises with my class, when two men in dark suits came into the gym. They spoke to my teacher, who summoned me. "Eva, you have to go to the administration building with these men. They are from the Department of Justice and they want to talk to you." This couldn't be good. "I can't go in my gym suit!" I said. "Get dressed," one of the men said gruffly, "and we'll walk you over there."

Once in an office alone with me, the two began to interrogate me harshly. "So you are in the habit of receiving subversive literature! Who else do you associate with that reads it?" I can defend myself, I thought with some patched-together confidence.

"I don't care about subversive literature, I'm just a seventeen-year-old freshman!" "Are you aware that the newsletters you received come from a Communist organization on the attorney general's list? Why did you ask for them?" I was going to straighten these goons out. "First of all, I'd be glad to explain the difference between Communists and other political groups," I said. "Secondly, I didn't ask for any newsletters. I'm the chairman of the Peace Club and people just send me stuff." "A likely story. Do you realize that distributing subversive materials is called sedition in this country? You're a naturalized citizen, aren't you?" "Yes." "Well, if you were found guilty of sedition, you could be de-naturalized!" My heart flipped over and headed toward my stomach. Denaturalized! I was so proud of being an American, and it had never occurred to me that my citizenship was second-class and could be taken away! My parents would kill me!

One of the men shifted in his chair and began to use a different tone. "On the other hand, if you give us a list of the Communists on this campus, perhaps we could overlook this..." I was almost too upset to talk, but I managed to say, "I don't know any Communists, and I'm not one myself." The truth was, I did know a few Communists, whom I considered to be misguided idealists. I also knew who Senator McCarthy was, and considered him a fascist. I had not expected to meet his henchmen.

"EVERYONE IS A LITTLE SUBVERSIVE BUT THEE AND ME, AND SOMETIMES I THINK EVEN THEE—,"

The men droned on with their questions, and finally left. Once they were out of sight I was in tears, having flashbacks of life in Vienna in 1938. Here I was in "the land of the free," an American now, being terrorized in 1953!

I rushed to the bathroom to wash my face and try to cool down. When I could think again, I decided to consult the college dean, J.D. Dawson. He was known to be a good man to talk with about a problem. I walked right into his office on the same floor and told him what had just happened. "Who allowed these men to interrogate you **in our college building?**" he thundered.

"Don't you worry, I'm not going to let anything happen to you. In fact, I'm going to send you to the best civil liberties lawyer to see what's what!" He picked up the telephone and dialed the attorney, who, surprisingly, was available right away. When he hung up, I had an appointment in two days in Washington D.C. "I don't have money for this," I said, very uncertain that my parents would go along with his plan. "Oh no, this is the fault of the college. We'll pay your bus fare, get you a hotel room and have this all straightened out." For just one moment, I wished J.D. was my father.

When I got to Washington, things went just as J.D. predicted. The attorney chuckled at the sight of me, a teenager in bobby sox being considered an enemy of the state. It turned out that the man who had sent me the newspapers was this attorney's client who was under investigation himself. "When the McCarthyites are serious about a prosecution, they make sure that no passport is issued," explained the attorney. "So I want you to apply for a passport and have your roommate apply on the same day. Call me and tell me when you get the passport — I'm sure you will, honey!"

And so my new roommate Jackie and I applied for passports the following week. She got hers in a month and I got mine in two months. Just as I expected, my mother was hysterical about the investigation, warning me over the phone never to do anything political ever again, angry that I had somehow put my whole family in danger, and so forth — but I weathered the storm. Through J.D., I had finally learned what it felt like to be fully supported.

Dreams and Hopes
New York

MY DREAM CAME TRUE! When I came to New York for an Antioch co-op job in the fall quarter I found an apartment of my own with a classmate, right in Greenwich Village. Annie and I located a sublet in the *Village Voice* newspaper — for $19 a month! There was a bathtub in the kitchen, but you could put a cover down over it and have counter space for preparing supper. This led to her drawing a cartoon with my caption: "I need a bath — the carrots can wait!" Downstairs on the first floor was an Italian men's social club. All we knew about it was that a bunch of old men were talking and playing cards there. They seemed to keep an eye on us to see that we were all right, since we looked so young.

We couldn't afford a phone, but there was one outside the corner store. I called my parents once a week and usually had to listen to a tirade about my choice not to live at home. Why would I want to live away from my parents, when I had a beautiful room in an apartment on Fifth Avenue? What was I up to, anyway? They couldn't understand that I had already lived like an adult at fifteen, and this wasn't a big change. Nor would it be easy to overcome the memories of my suffering in that apartment, even with my brother in the hospital now.

My parents calmed down a bit as Annie and I began to visit them once a week for dinner, and I actually enjoyed being a "guest." Annie and I gave many parties in our apartment with my writer friends from Bronx Science and our folk-singing friends from Antioch who were also on New York jobs. We hardly dated any guys and when we did, it was to go browsing in a bookstore or have coffee at Café Rienzi and view the Village scene of artists and poets.

That fall I worked at the Hospital for Joint Diseases in East Harlem. My job was to interview new patients at the clinic and determine their fee levels and which specialist they needed. I picked up a little Spanish from interviewing Puerto Rican patients, and learned southern dialects from the black Harlem residents. There was also a sprinkling of elderly Russian Jews in the neighborhood, usually suffering from severe arthritis with complaints such as "I can't stand up, I can't sit down, and I can't lie down." In a day at the clinic, I might meet a heroin addict, a victim of domestic violence, or a parent with a handicapped child.

I loved working with people and being involved in delivering services to them. What I didn't like was the hospital atmosphere with its strict stratification: the male doctors at the top of the hierarchy, the women workers undervalued. I also had no wish to relate with my co-workers because of their constant snide gossip about each other and the doctors. I tried to console myself by remembering that this was just what a co-op job was about — sorting out what I wanted and didn't want in a career someday.

Before I left New York I had a terrible visit with my brother. My mother told me that he missed me and I should go to the hospital to see him. I felt so very sad for him, knowing how frightened and angry he must have been, locked up in a psychiatric unit against his will — yet I believed neither of us was ready for a visit. Mother kept insisting, and I finally took a train upstate and a taxi to the hospital. The huge size of the place and its wooded terrain were awe inspiring, but not in a good way. At first Helmut was glad to see me and to confide his complaints. But when I took a walk with him around the grounds he became agitated and punched my arm very hard. When I returned to my mother's apartment I started sobbing. She revealed, "Well, his doctor told me not to send you, but I thought it was a good idea, myself." She didn't even apologize. Now the limited trust that I had in her was gone.

There was no one except my therapist Joan to whom I could talk about my pain after this. It terrified me to think of going back to the life I used to have when I couldn't protect myself. I knew I had to cling to my goals and keep from moving backwards at any cost.

When it was time to return to Antioch in October, Annie kept our apartment and dropped out of school. It was hard for me to leave my Greenwich Village haven. But when I went back to college I felt at home there, too. And I couldn't wait to take the class called "Self and Society," which would help me make sense of the many issues I'd been observing on my job.

Romance and Reality

Philadelphia, PA

O N AND OFF, I'd been dating a young man I had gotten to know through my activist work. He attended college near Philadelphia and I had hopes of seeing him more often. When a co-op job assisting a kindergarten teacher became available in that region, I grabbed it. In between my work hours and his study hours, we somehow managed to find time to be together. We would listen to a band at a jazz club or to folk records at my apartment and talk late into the night. We were able to talk to each other about hidden fears, which I couldn't do with anyone else. Our relationship became intense and I was full of daydreams. I imagined a long-term romance in which we gave each other constant moral support, regardless of distance. It was jarring and hurtful to me when my boyfriend announced his point of view that "fidelity is impossible." Still, I couldn't really believe that I would never come first for him the way he did for me.

One evening, I visited his college in secret. Hiding in the shadows, I saw for myself how involved he was with someone else. Finally I understood that I had to end the relationship.

I returned to Antioch with an aching heart, but also a voice in my head telling me, "Time to get real, girl!" My friends Paula, Mitzi, Judy, Joy and Footsie (yes, that was her name) helped me overcome this time of sadness and disappointment. I couldn't stop thinking about how hard it would be when I graduated, letting go of these precious friendships as we all moved in different directions. Would I end up completely alone?

Fortunately, the classes I took in my junior year were absorbing and fascinating. This helped take my mind off my sense of loss. I especially liked a research project in my sociology class. We were doing a large survey of the political attitudes of people in rural southwestern Ohio. My classmates and I fanned out to interview farmers, industrial workers, professors and housewives for the study. I was most intrigued by their varying opinions about what our government should be doing.

In my psychology class I was starting to sort out my own complicated feelings about psychoanalysis. Until now I had not appreciated the value of attending lectures with my parents and meeting their colleagues who were leaders in the field, like Viktor Frankl, Alexandra Adler (the daughter of Alfred Adler), Karen Horney, and others. In fact, this had been an extraordinary education without my realizing it. Now, in my college class we were studying Freud and those who followed him. I began to understand that the psychoanalytic revolution made it possible to explore human motives and actions in depth. I was hungry to learn more. I hoped I could use new methods for relieving personal suffering in my future work.

Literature classes made me feel restless, especially lengthy book critiques. But reading novels on my own gave me great pleasure and relaxation. Sometimes I took lessons from these books on how to be an American girl. Now I was considering one of the things I had read: when an American girl has a broken heart, the thing to do is to go on a trip to Europe.

He's The One!

Europe

I WAS BUSY NOW, planning a summer trip to Europe. My mother objected, without giving any clear reasons. Since I had saved my own money from one of my jobs and an insurance claim, and could swing it myself, she finally consented. My history professor, Irwin Abrams, encouraged me to go, not as a tourist but with the purpose of contributing in some way. I applied to a program sponsored by the American Friends Service Committee in which a group of American students were volunteering at various international work camps. Many European countries were still struggling with post-war recovery and we would join in to help. The college agreed to give me work credits for such a trip.

When my acceptance letter came, it mentioned that Hank Maiden, my friend from Antioch, would be attending the same program as part of his alternative service as a conscientious objector. What good news! I remembered the wide smile Hank often flashed and the light that came from his blue eyes. Too bad he was so short!

Hank soon arrived at our college town in Ohio on

135

his way across the country from the west coast and called me up. We met for pizza and a beer, each on a date with someone else. After some lively conversation he took us all in his rattly wooden station wagon with a missing window, and dropped the others off. It seemed he and I both knew we'd rather be alone together. Sitting in front of my dormitory on top of a concrete bicycle rack, we were eager to catch up on our time apart. Hank told stories of his alternative service job in California sending relief packages to Korea instead of fighting in the war. I spoke of my studies, and about the mixed feelings I had about returning to visit Austria soon. The next day he drove to the east coast, and I continued my classes.

When my school year was over, I was glad to get to Pendle Hill, the Quaker retreat center near Philadelphia. There our small group of idealistic students would prepare for the summer in Europe. It was great to see Hank again.

One afternoon, I invited Hank to visit the private school in the next town, where I had been an assistant kindergarten teacher on my previous co-op job. As we hiked on a path through the woods, Hank told me of his yearning to build a family. With most of his five brothers and sisters already married, he felt strongly about this, though he wasn't sure what work he would do in the future. I confided that I wanted to be a psychologist, and to raise a family someday. I wished I could figure out how to put it together. He pictured a full partnership, he said, which would involve a man doing just as much parenting and housework as a woman. Both would be activists for peace and a better world. I was thrilled with his ideas. It was the first time I could envision the kind of life I would want in a marriage. What difference did it make that he was shorter than me? We were in step with each other as we walked, and could dream out loud together! Could I dare to hope that we would be a couple?

By the time we were boarding a student ship in Canada, it was accepted by our group that Hank and I were "going together." There was a problem, though, that almost kept him from sailing — he was short of money to pay the fare! He boldly asked to speak to the captain, and offered his services in any possible way to make up the difference. Happily, there was a vacancy for an assistant night watch-man, and he took it.

By day we attended classes aboard ship, to pre-pare us for working with different cultures. At night we prowled the ship together as Hank shone his huge flashlight around. I really enjoyed being the as-sistant to the assistant night watchman! The ship's crew spoke German, and I translated their conver-sations for Hank. There was plenty of time for long talks, especially about Gandhi, the great teacher of non-violent world strategies. And there was time for passionate kisses in our quiet moments on deck.

After ten days at sea I disembarked in Ireland, the ship's first port, to travel to a work project near Belfast. There, we made physical improvements to a Waldorf school for retarded children. It was staffed by Christian exiles from Nazi Germany who practiced Rudolf Steiner's "anthroposophy." One day, when we were building a sea wall in drizzling weather, Sami from Lebanon noticed that I was getting very chilled. Without asking me, he took off his green shirt and threw it over my shoulders. "Just keep this," he said. How amazing for me, as a Jew, to have an Arab friend! It really changed my perspective.

Hank was able to visit me at the school, taking a weekend off from his own work camp in England. My new friends were impressed with his strength and good cheer as he helped us bring in the hay for the school's horses. Later Hank and I talked about his upcoming trial in the fall for taking part in a demonstration. During the previous spring, New York City had declared its first A-bomb shelter drill. Hank and a small group of protesters sat on benches in New York's City Hall Park, refusing to take shelter. The police arrested twenty-nine paci-fists and an Italian-speaking shoeshine man who happened to be working in the park. They were re-leased, with orders to stand trial later.

When it was time for Hank to return to Eng-land, I was worrying about the outcome of his trial, but didn't want to show it. Hank and I had a tender parting and hoped for another rendezvous soon.

I had signed on for several projects and my next assignment was in Holland. An international youth team was rebuilding a park that had been sabotaged by the Dutch underground to slow down the advance of German tanks. Our accommodations were very simple, including an outhouse labeled "International Peace Palace." We worked outdoors in our short pants and sweaty T-shirts, improving the paths and tilling the soil to restore the gardens at the park. Passing truck drivers whistled at the girls and honked their horns. Fortunately there were a number of Dutch boys in the project providing friendship and protection.

Towards the end of the project, a cable arrived for me from Italy, where Hank was working at the time: "PLEASE JOIN ME IN PARIS. DEPARTING FOR NEW YORK SOON FOR TRIAL." Of course I would join him! My next and last work assignment was to be in Salzburg, Austria, and I rushed to study the train schedule for a route that would take me through Paris. I returned the cable and was soon on a train headed for a rendezvous with Hank. We planned to sightsee and have a sentimental farewell for an indefinite time apart — depending on the outcome of his trial. We shared just a few beautiful days in Paris, and they brought us closer, as I had hoped.

Afterwards, riding on the Orient Express train

to Salzburg I cried for a long time. How long would the two of us be separated now? Troubling thoughts kept repeating themselves in rhythm with the train's wheels. But once I arrived at the work project and joined in, I was able to change my focus.

In Salzburg, my group served as day-camp counselors at a community center for "Americanization" of local kids. The American occupation army had developed the center hoping to bring about attitude changes among Austria's youth after their exposure to Nazi propaganda. At first I was proud of my fluent, if childlike, German-speaking ability, but then the children said "Tante Eva sure talks funny." I was, after all, an American girl now, even in the way I spoke German. And yet — there were moments when I felt quite at home in Austria.

The evenings were free for long group discussions about world affairs and our home countries. It was intriguing to meet Austrian college students. There was even a pleasant girl my age, also named Eva, who was a pre-med student at University of Vienna. I was surprised to hear her say, "I get along fine with Jewish people at school — but why do the Jewish guys always want to date white girls?" There was plenty of lingering anti-Semitism in Europe, yet it shocked me to hear this from a fellow volunteer.

I was going to hate leaving the beautiful city of Salzburg, but I was anxious to reach the last destination on my trip. This time it was not for a work assignment. I would be going on my own to visit Vienna, city of my family's most endearing memories and worst nightmares.

Return to Vienna

August, 1955

.

T HE STREETCAR LURCHED, and I almost lost my footing. I was making my way to the home my family had lived in, before we had to escape to save our lives. Although I had been a small child then, the buildings and trees I saw from the tram window seemed slightly familiar. So many memories pushed into my mind as we moved along the tracks. I remembered the smell of Nivea Cream in our nursery — and how I used to like watching my older brother Helmut play with his friends, laughing. In those days he didn't have the angry, frightened expression that repelled people now. Thinking about him, I remembered the uniforms and boots of German soldiers, but not their faces. My heart began to beat stronger and faster.

As I hung onto the streetcar pole, the tune of "Vienna, City of My Dreams" repeated itself in my mind with hollow chords. I watched passing street signs, looking for Taborstrasse where we had lived. It was only when I saw the leather shop at the front of our apartment building that I realized it was time to get off. Yes, there above the shop was the balcony my mother was so proud of. It looked smaller than it should have been — back in New York she still spoke of it as being quite grand. Walking slowly toward the window of the leather shop, I thought this must have been where my mother bought her beautiful gloves, and my father his briefcase. I wondered crazily how a store could continue to exist when those who tended it had vanished.

It was important to calm myself now for my meeting with Chnava, the *Hausbesorger* (building manager). My father had explained to me that Chnava was a Czech who was anti-Nazi, and had done what he could for the Jewish families who once inhabited the entire building.

My brother had sailed to Europe on a student ship some years earlier while on a college break, and had spoken with Chnava. Helmut was given two carefully saved letters addressed to my mother in 1941 and 1942. Each one was from the German government, informing my mother that a sister of hers had perished. The letters didn't mention **how** the sisters had been murdered. When my brother brought the letters back to New York, they reminded me of a wartime movie in which an American family received a Western Union telegram during the war: "We regret to inform you that your son..." Except, the German letters didn't contain the regret part.

Walking into the building, I had no trouble finding Chnava's door on the first floor. We embraced happily as the old man gushed in Viennese dialect with a Czech accent — what a cute little girl I had been, and here I was now, a grown young lady, a college student! He had already seen someone from almost every family, he said, as the survivors came to visit from many lands. In fact, my brother had come, did I know that? What a difficult child he had been! Many a time, Chnava remembered, our nanny had to struggle with him at the staircase when he had a tantrum. Would I like to walk through the building so that he could tell me about the families that used to live here? His voice was warm and sympathetic. We both understood that such a tour would mean visiting ghosts.

We first stopped at the door opposite mine. "*N'ja*, the Weinbergs, they escaped to Shanghai," Chnava began. "And here's your apartment, one of the biggest in the building. What a busy place it was, with your father's and mother's patients coming in and out all day! By the time your parents left with you kids, and that bitch of a woman, that Nazi doctor took it over, there wasn't too much going on anymore!"

We climbed another flight, and stopped in front of each door. "Ja, the Gerstingers — the S.S. came before dawn one day — they sent the father to Dachau, but the teenage boy, he wasn't home that night. He came alone to visit after the war. And the Lindemanns, this is their door — they were from

South America, they managed to get back there before it was too late. Do you remember, Emmanuelito
used to play with Helmut? You kids called him Lito.
And here were the Schwartz's — the father got tak-
en somewhere by the S.S. right away back in 1938
— they were a big family but their mother got all the
kids out with her to France...after that I don't know
what happened. Evalein, is Pittsburgh very far from
New York? Here, you see, this is where Herr and
Frau Gottesmann used to live — they visited five
years ago from Pittsburgh."

Another flight of steps. "Well, the Lederers — it
was no good at all — they ended up in Auschwitz,
the whole bunch. And the Klein family — she never
left Vienna. After they sent her man to Germany
and worked him to death she just moved to a different district with identity papers as a Catholic for
herself and the little girl. I think her sister was married to a Catholic."

My tears stayed on the inside, as we returned
down the stairs. I already knew that I had lost a
home and a safe childhood. But now I felt a new
loss. All of the families around us had been a part
of me once.

I told Chnava a few stories of my family's life in
America, and we parted with another hug. When I
stepped outside, the glare of the sun hurt my eyes
after our dark tour. There was still one bombed-out
building on the block, and I was somehow very glad

to see it. It was like a sculpture, expressing my feelings. And seeing it, I thought maybe my neighbors wouldn't be forgotten so easily.

In reconstructing the conversation above, I have fictionalized the names and some of the destinations of my former neighbors. Their fates tell the story of the murderous era of Nazi domination in Austria.

Back to New York

WHEN I CAME BACK from my volunteer work to my parents' apartment in late September, I had several different infections. I didn't complain at the time, but the meals on my work projects had been scant, sometimes not much more than bread and tea. I had already been malnourished in the days of our escape from Vienna, and I guess my body wasn't ready for another round of scarcity.

My parents were indulgent while I was ill. My father sent me to various specialists, a different Viennese refugee doctor for each of my infections. The trouble with these medical visits was, I was still afraid of men with German accents. As I slowly began to recover I suspected it was from eating Aunt Valli's delicious meals again, not because of their antibiotics.

Hank visited the apartment often between meetings with lawyers about his coming trial. It was still unclear what the consequence would be for resisting the atomic bomb shelter drill last spring.

"What are you doing with a jailbird?" my mother said. Mother was an arrow looking for a target, and she hit a bull's eye with him. "I love a man who follows his principles," I said. "You're a doctor and you know that there is no such thing as a shelter from A-bombs."

The trial date turned into a postponement, and it looked as if Hank would have to come to New York all over again to face a possible jail sentence. This would spoil his plan to return to Antioch and graduate by next summer. We were eager to be together, and he came up with a solution. When I returned for the upcoming college quarter, he would follow me to Yellow Springs and work as a carpenter's apprentice.

"What are you doing with a college dropout?" my mother asked. "He'll enroll again when his trial is over," I said. "And besides that, he's a *goy* (non-Jew)," my mother said. I replied "He may not be Jewish, but I'm no less of a Jew than I was before."

At last it was time to return to Antioch in October. I was able to enjoy good friends and interesting psychology classes. Hank lived near the college campus, and often joined our activities when he finished his day's work. Time seemed to move very fast until winter vacation. I was leaving soon to visit my parents and my aunt for a week in New York.

On a phone call before I arrived my mother said "Don't mention the name of the jailbird when you come! I've arranged a date for you with a nice navy captain who's Jewish — it can't hurt, and you should be seeing other 'prospects'." Musically, my mother couldn't carry a tune — and she certainly was out of tune with me. As for her objection to my dating a non-Jew, I could sympathize a little. At least in this particular respect she was doing what Jewish mothers are expected to do, trying to ensure that her child would hold onto the religion and culture of the family.

Although I was delighted to see my dad and my aunt, the week away from Yellow Springs dragged along very slowly. I even went out on the date that was set up with the guy whom I privately dubbed "Captain *Boychik*" (Yiddish for "young man"). He sensed my lack of interest but was very polite, and my mother was temporarily pacified.

I came back to Ohio with depleted energy and low spirits. Hank's face showed me right away that he felt utterly discouraged by my mother's disapproval. On top of that, he had been told there would not be enough work for him in the winter season. He decided to go home to his parents who lived across Puget Sound from Seattle. I had made a commitment to work in the college library for the winter quarter, as I didn't feel up to taking on difficult challenges after my recent illnesses. When we spoke of the prospect of parting till spring, we both began to cry.

My rented room in town felt like a very lonely place after Hank left and my friends were on other jobs out of town. Everything I wanted was on hold: my relationship with my boyfriend, my support

149

system, progress in my career. Were my goals even possible? I went to my library job every day for a month without enthusiasm.

When one of my infections recurred I quit my job, and my supervisor didn't seem to mind at all. A blizzard was blowing into town as I struggled to carry a large stack of books from the library to my room in preparation for a long convalescence. And then Hank called me up.

"The weather's great on the West Coast! You could recover better here. Why don't you fly out and meet my family? Dad has plenty of work for me here right now. For your last semester I'll drive us back to Yellow Springs in the station wagon." "I couldn't do that," I said — "unless maybe we were engaged..." And then he proposed to me and I accepted!

Calling my parents was scary and difficult. "I wish you a lot of happiness," said my father and passed the phone to my mother. Her response was: "If you can't be talked out of this engagement I will *sit shiva* for you." (Sitting shiva is a Jewish ritual of mourning for the dead.) I knew this occurred among Orthodox Jews — but we weren't Orthodox! "I'm very much alive, I love you both, and I'm going to Washington," I said. As soon as I hung up, though, I couldn't stop crying, devastated by the thought of having no family anymore.

I consulted the college psychologist, who helped me regain some perspective and was even optimistic that my mother's attitude would change over time. My faculty adviser's opinion was that I was doing well by choosing a more balanced life. He said he had once been concerned that I was too driven and might be headed for a successful career without personal happiness. Besides, he pointed out, it was quite normal for girls in the class of 1957 to be marrying around the time of graduation.

I was soon on the plane to Seattle, slightly feverish. Hank met my plane with the biggest smile I had ever seen. After we took a ferry across Puget Sound and drove to his home, his parents gave me a warm welcome.

Over the next month they made sure I had a good rest in their old-fashioned country home. His mother taught me how to make fruit pies. His dad told me stories of the family's life on their farm in Iowa before the war. When he got to know me, he said, "Any New York girl who flies here to be with my son oughta marry him soon!" As I got stronger, I began to visit his brothers and sisters nearby. Was it really true that I would have a big American family now? I could hardly believe it, and felt very pleased and a little overwhelmed. And then it was time to return to college for the spring term.

From College to "Adult Life"

Yellow Springs, Ohio — 1956

M Y VERY LAST college class ended on a hot day in June. I had finished five years' academic work in four. For graduation, the college still required me to get three more months of work credits and write a paper on my philosophy of life.

I felt wonderful as I sat on a rocking chair on the front porch of my summer apartment, listening to the crickets. All my thoughts were about the future. Hank and I were planning our wedding for the end of August at the college chapel. I ran a mental preview of the whole event and smiled from deep inside. I would wear a pastel cocktail dress and ballerina flats. Friends would be coming back to town from their co-op jobs and would join us for the wedding. It had taken months of dealing with my mother's hostile resistance, but she had finally agreed to come. That meant my father and aunt would be there, too. Hank's Aunt Lillian, a retired teacher from Cleveland, would represent the Maidens.

The next week I would be starting a social work job at the Department of Welfare in Dayton, Ohio. How delightful that I could stay on in Yellow Springs, my adopted hometown, a while longer when Hank returned to college! Our plan after that was to settle in the San Francisco Bay Area — a region of great beauty, fine climate, and an atmosphere conducive to social change. I pictured us in a cozy apartment with friends streaming in and out.

First Hank would get his degree in sociology while I supported both of us. Then I would get a graduate degree in psychology and work with whatever children had the greatest need. We would attend Quaker meetings, especially for the benefits of meditation, which had a very calming effect on me. We would also observe Jewish holidays and customs. We would work for peace and social justice together. And we would be very devoted parents when the time came.

There were still many obstacles to overcome. It was true that we were starting out very young without any financial security. And we did come from extremely different backgrounds. My mother's criticisms and advice weren't necessarily wrong — just delivered in a hurtful, unsupportive way. At least by now I knew how to find or create support systems for myself.

Fortunately, my brother's mental health was improving. He was on a new psychiatric medication, and was traveling in Europe after his long hospital stay. He would probably live in my parents' apartment in New York when he returned. I planned to keep in touch with him and my parents — but from a distance.

Jumping off the porch, I biked over to Hank's apartment to pick him up for a couple of end-of-school parties. Despite the heat, I felt a breeze on my face as I pedaled fast, full of a sense of freedom I had never felt before.

Afterword

OVER THE NEXT SIX YEARS, we settled in the San Francisco Bay area. Hank got his degree in sociology from the University of California and began to work in the book business. Our two sons were born, to our great delight. While working as a preschool teacher, I entered a graduate program in psychology.

The years of raising my two children were the most satisfying time in my life. My pleasure in their activities and unique personalities gave me a second chance to enjoy childhood, this time from a parent's point of view. Our very full lives included an annual trip to see the large Maiden family in rural Washington, and another to visit my family in New York City.

My studies and work were on a part-time schedule while my sons were growing up. As a school psychologist, I chose to work in districts that served low-income families, where I could make more of a difference. I enjoyed being part of a team to provide special education and other needed services. Meanwhile I took special training in family therapy. When my children were in college I established my own private practice in psychotherapy. My interest in teamwork led to founding a mental health clinic linked with a medical practice in Palo Alto. This work was also satisfying and challenging.

My husband and I continued to be activists. When the draft for the Vietnam War began, we took a stand against it and educated young men on their options. Opposition to nuclear testing and supporting equal rights for women were also areas of social action.

I lost my father in a street accident, but not before he had known his grandchildren, who added joy to his life. How he loved playing chess with them!

My brother became multilingual, achieving mastery of seven languages. He was stable when he had effective medication, a good psychotherapist, a calm routine, and safe housing. We were all able to enjoy his prolific intellect and sense of humor at those times.

During the final illnesses of my mother and brother, I was their caregiver – sometimes close by, sometimes from a distance. All of the love we felt was expressed and completed during those last days together.

My aunt Valli lived to the age of 91. She had been trained as a high school teacher of Latin and Greek. Instead of continuing on that path, she had given most of her life to living with us and helping in every way possible.

When my original family was no longer living I felt a need to understand our shared history in

Europe on my own terms. I joined a support group of holocaust survivors who were children in wartime. I hoped to reduce the lingering distress I felt when difficult memories came up. The group experience was helpful for me. Those of us trained in mental health decided to help isolated older survivors and began to organize social programs and counseling services in several communities. This work led to my meeting many courageous people. Eventually existing agencies picked up the work that we started.

Today I am a contented mother, grandmother, and writer. I start each day with a meditation to clear my mind and "count my blessings," which are plentiful.

Acknowledgements

I am filled with gratitude to all those who assisted me with this book. This includes my dedicated writing teachers, Elaine Starkman, Sheila Dunec, and Meredith Paige; editors Anne Grenn Saldinger, Ben Maiden, and Lisa Sousa; and publishing guru Mark Weiman. I was also fortunate to have the help of wonderful artists. Mariana Silverman (age 16) made the drawings; Colleen Sterling inked them; Peter Maiden consulted on photos; and Paul Veres designed the cover.

Thanks to all, for efforts that came from the heart!

Made in the USA
Charleston, SC
21 April 2014